C-4006   CAREER EXAMINATION SERIES

This is your
PASSBOOK for...

Job Opportunity Specialist

Test Preparation Study Guide
Questions & Answers

COPYRIGHT NOTICE

This book is SOLELY intended for, is sold ONLY to, and its use is RESTRICTED to individual, bona fide applicants or candidates who qualify by virtue of having seriously filed applications for appropriate license, certificate, professional and/or promotional advancement, higher school matriculation, scholarship, or other legitimate requirements of education and/or governmental authorities.

This book is NOT intended for use, class instruction, tutoring, training, duplication, copying, reprinting, excerption, or adaptation, etc., by:

1) Other publishers
2) Proprietors and/or Instructors of "Coaching" and/or Preparatory Courses
3) Personnel and/or Training Divisions of commercial, industrial, and governmental organizations
4) Schools, colleges, or universities and/or their departments and staffs, including teachers and other personnel
5) Testing Agencies or Bureaus
6) Study groups which seek by the purchase of a single volume to copy and/or duplicate and/or adapt this material for use by the group as a whole without having purchased individual volumes for each of the members of the group
7) Et al.

Such persons would be in violation of appropriate Federal and State statutes.

PROVISION OF LICENSING AGREEMENTS – Recognized educational, commercial, industrial, and governmental institutions and organizations, and others legitimately engaged in educational pursuits, including training, testing, and measurement activities, may address request for a licensing agreement to the copyright owners, who will determine whether, and under what conditions, including fees and charges, the materials in this book may be used them. In other words, a licensing facility exists for the legitimate use of the material in this book on other than an individual basis. However, it is asseverated and affirmed here that the material in this book CANNOT be used without the receipt of the express permission of such a licensing agreement from the Publishers. Inquiries re licensing should be addressed to the company, attention rights and permissions department.

All rights reserved, including the right of reproduction in whole or in part, in any form or by any means, electronic or mechanical, including photocopying, recording, or by any information storage and retrieval system, without permission in writing from the Publisher.

Copyright © 2024 by
National Learning Corporation

212 Michael Drive, Syosset, NY 11791
(516) 921-8888 • www.passbooks.com
E-mail: info@passbooks.com

PUBLISHED IN THE UNITED STATES OF AMERICA

PASSBOOK® SERIES

THE *PASSBOOK® SERIES* has been created to prepare applicants and candidates for the ultimate academic battlefield – the examination room.

At some time in our lives, each and every one of us may be required to take an examination – for validation, matriculation, admission, qualification, registration, certification, or licensure.

Based on the assumption that every applicant or candidate has met the basic formal educational standards, has taken the required number of courses, and read the necessary texts, the *PASSBOOK® SERIES* furnishes the one special preparation which may assure passing with confidence, instead of failing with insecurity. Examination questions – together with answers – are furnished as the basic vehicle for study so that the mysteries of the examination and its compounding difficulties may be eliminated or diminished by a sure method.

This book is meant to help you pass your examination provided that you qualify and are serious in your objective.

The entire field is reviewed through the huge store of content information which is succinctly presented through a provocative and challenging approach – the question-and-answer method.

A climate of success is established by furnishing the correct answers at the end of each test.

You soon learn to recognize types of questions, forms of questions, and patterns of questioning. You may even begin to anticipate expected outcomes.

You perceive that many questions are repeated or adapted so that you can gain acute insights, which may enable you to score many sure points.

You learn how to confront new questions, or types of questions, and to attack them confidently and work out the correct answers.

You note objectives and emphases, and recognize pitfalls and dangers, so that you may make positive educational adjustments.

Moreover, you are kept fully informed in relation to new concepts, methods, practices, and directions in the field.

You discover that you are actually taking the examination all the time: you are preparing for the examination by "taking" an examination, not by reading extraneous and/or supererogatory textbooks.

In short, this PASSBOOK®, used directedly, should be an important factor in helping you to pass your test.

JOB OPPORTUNITY SPECIALIST

DUTIES
Job Opportunity Specialists, under supervision, with some latitude for independent judgment and decision making and in accordance with agency policies/procedures and federal/state regulations, provide economic support and employment related services to persons in need, to promote individual and family self-sufficiency; perform related work.

SCOPE OF THE EXAMINATION
The <u>written test</u> will be multiple-choice and is designed to test for knowledge, skills and/or abilities in: written expression; interviewing techniques; decision making; prioritizing; the ability to recognize the feelings, needs, and points of view of others and to modify one's approach to most effectively meet the needs of a situation; problem recognition; applying procedures to specific problems; synthesizing information; basic arithmetic; and other related areas.

HOW TO TAKE A TEST

I. YOU MUST PASS AN EXAMINATION

A. WHAT EVERY CANDIDATE SHOULD KNOW

Examination applicants often ask us for help in preparing for the written test. What can I study in advance? What kinds of questions will be asked? How will the test be given? How will the papers be graded?

As an applicant for a civil service examination, you may be wondering about some of these things. Our purpose here is to suggest effective methods of advance study and to describe civil service examinations.

Your chances for success on this examination can be increased if you know how to prepare. Those "pre-examination jitters" can be reduced if you know what to expect. You can even experience an adventure in good citizenship if you know why civil service exams are given.

B. WHY ARE CIVIL SERVICE EXAMINATIONS GIVEN?

Civil service examinations are important to you in two ways. As a citizen, you want public jobs filled by employees who know how to do their work. As a job seeker, you want a fair chance to compete for that job on an equal footing with other candidates. The best-known means of accomplishing this two-fold goal is the competitive examination.

Exams are widely publicized throughout the nation. They may be administered for jobs in federal, state, city, municipal, town or village governments or agencies.

Any citizen may apply, with some limitations, such as the age or residence of applicants. Your experience and education may be reviewed to see whether you meet the requirements for the particular examination. When these requirements exist, they are reasonable and applied consistently to all applicants. Thus, a competitive examination may cause you some uneasiness now, but it is your privilege and safeguard.

C. HOW ARE CIVIL SERVICE EXAMS DEVELOPED?

Examinations are carefully written by trained technicians who are specialists in the field known as "psychological measurement," in consultation with recognized authorities in the field of work that the test will cover. These experts recommend the subject matter areas or skills to be tested; only those knowledges or skills important to your success on the job are included. The most reliable books and source materials available are used as references. Together, the experts and technicians judge the difficulty level of the questions.

Test technicians know how to phrase questions so that the problem is clearly stated. Their ethics do not permit "trick" or "catch" questions. Questions may have been tried out on sample groups, or subjected to statistical analysis, to determine their usefulness.

Written tests are often used in combination with performance tests, ratings of training and experience, and oral interviews. All of these measures combine to form the best-known means of finding the right person for the right job.

II. HOW TO PASS THE WRITTEN TEST

A. NATURE OF THE EXAMINATION

To prepare intelligently for civil service examinations, you should know how they differ from school examinations you have taken. In school you were assigned certain definite pages to read or subjects to cover. The examination questions were quite detailed and usually emphasized memory. Civil service exams, on the other hand, try to discover your present ability to perform the duties of a position, plus your potentiality to learn these duties. In other words, a civil service exam attempts to predict how successful you will be. Questions cover such a broad area that they cannot be as minute and detailed as school exam questions.

In the public service similar kinds of work, or positions, are grouped together in one "class." This process is known as *position-classification*. All the positions in a class are paid according to the salary range for that class. One class title covers all of these positions, and they are all tested by the same examination.

B. FOUR BASIC STEPS

1) Study the announcement

How, then, can you know what subjects to study? Our best answer is: "Learn as much as possible about the class of positions for which you've applied." The exam will test the knowledge, skills and abilities needed to do the work.

Your most valuable source of information about the position you want is the official exam announcement. This announcement lists the training and experience qualifications. Check these standards and apply only if you come reasonably close to meeting them.

The brief description of the position in the examination announcement offers some clues to the subjects which will be tested. Think about the job itself. Review the duties in your mind. Can you perform them, or are there some in which you are rusty? Fill in the blank spots in your preparation.

Many jurisdictions preview the written test in the exam announcement by including a section called "Knowledge and Abilities Required," "Scope of the Examination," or some similar heading. Here you will find out specifically what fields will be tested.

2) Review your own background

Once you learn in general what the position is all about, and what you need to know to do the work, ask yourself which subjects you already know fairly well and which need improvement. You may wonder whether to concentrate on improving your strong areas or on building some background in your fields of weakness. When the announcement has specified "some knowledge" or "considerable knowledge," or has used adjectives like "beginning principles of…" or "advanced … methods," you can get a clue as to the number and difficulty of questions to be asked in any given field. More questions, and hence broader coverage, would be included for those subjects which are more important in the work. Now weigh your strengths and weaknesses against the job requirements and prepare accordingly.

3) Determine the level of the position

Another way to tell how intensively you should prepare is to understand the level of the job for which you are applying. Is it the entering level? In other words, is this the position in which beginners in a field of work are hired? Or is it an intermediate or advanced level? Sometimes this is indicated by such words as "Junior" or "Senior" in the class title. Other jurisdictions use Roman numerals to designate the level – Clerk I, Clerk II, for example. The word "Supervisor" sometimes appears in the title. If the level is not indicated by the title, check the description of duties. Will you be working under very close supervision, or will you have responsibility for independent decisions in this work?

4) Choose appropriate study materials

Now that you know the subjects to be examined and the relative amount of each subject to be covered, you can choose suitable study materials. For beginning level jobs, or even advanced ones, if you have a pronounced weakness in some aspect of your training, read a modern, standard textbook in that field. Be sure it is up to date and has general coverage. Such books are normally available at your library, and the librarian will be glad to help you locate one. For entry-level positions, questions of appropriate difficulty are chosen – neither highly advanced questions, nor those too simple. Such questions require careful thought but not advanced training.

If the position for which you are applying is technical or advanced, you will read more advanced, specialized material. If you are already familiar with the basic principles of your field, elementary textbooks would waste your time. Concentrate on advanced textbooks and technical periodicals. Think through the concepts and review difficult problems in your field.

These are all general sources. You can get more ideas on your own initiative, following these leads. For example, training manuals and publications of the government agency which employs workers in your field can be useful, particularly for technical and professional positions. A letter or visit to the government department involved may result in more specific study suggestions, and certainly will provide you with a more definite idea of the exact nature of the position you are seeking.

III. KINDS OF TESTS

Tests are used for purposes other than measuring knowledge and ability to perform specified duties. For some positions, it is equally important to test ability to make adjustments to new situations or to profit from training. In others, basic mental abilities not dependent on information are essential. Questions which test these things may not appear as pertinent to the duties of the position as those which test for knowledge and information. Yet they are often highly important parts of a fair examination. For very general questions, it is almost impossible to help you direct your study efforts. What we can do is to point out some of the more common of these general abilities needed in public service positions and describe some typical questions.

1) General information

Broad, general information has been found useful for predicting job success in some kinds of work. This is tested in a variety of ways, from vocabulary lists to questions about current events. Basic background in some field of work, such as sociology or economics, may be sampled in a group of questions. Often these are principles which have become familiar to most persons through exposure rather than through formal training. It is difficult to advise you how to study for these questions; being alert to the world around you is our best suggestion.

2) Verbal ability

An example of an ability needed in many positions is verbal or language ability. Verbal ability is, in brief, the ability to use and understand words. Vocabulary and grammar tests are typical measures of this ability. Reading comprehension or paragraph interpretation questions are common in many kinds of civil service tests. You are given a paragraph of written material and asked to find its central meaning.

3) Numerical ability

Number skills can be tested by the familiar arithmetic problem, by checking paired lists of numbers to see which are alike and which are different, or by interpreting charts and graphs. In the latter test, a graph may be printed in the test booklet which you are asked to use as the basis for answering questions.

4) Observation

A popular test for law-enforcement positions is the observation test. A picture is shown to you for several minutes, then taken away. Questions about the picture test your ability to observe both details and larger elements.

5) Following directions

In many positions in the public service, the employee must be able to carry out written instructions dependably and accurately. You may be given a chart with several columns, each column listing a variety of information. The questions require you to carry out directions involving the information given in the chart.

6) Skills and aptitudes

Performance tests effectively measure some manual skills and aptitudes. When the skill is one in which you are trained, such as typing or shorthand, you can practice. These tests are often very much like those given in business school or high school courses. For many of the other skills and aptitudes, however, no short-time preparation can be made. Skills and abilities natural to you or that you have developed throughout your lifetime are being tested.

Many of the general questions just described provide all the data needed to answer the questions and ask you to use your reasoning ability to find the answers. Your best preparation for these tests, as well as for tests of facts and ideas, is to be at your physical and mental best. You, no doubt, have your own methods of getting into an exam-taking mood and keeping "in shape." The next section lists some ideas on this subject.

IV. KINDS OF QUESTIONS

Only rarely is the "essay" question, which you answer in narrative form, used in civil service tests. Civil service tests are usually of the short-answer type. Full instructions for answering these questions will be given to you at the examination. But in case this is your first experience with short-answer questions and separate answer sheets, here is what you need to know:

1) Multiple-choice Questions

Most popular of the short-answer questions is the "multiple choice" or "best answer" question. It can be used, for example, to test for factual knowledge, ability to solve problems or judgment in meeting situations found at work.

A multiple-choice question is normally one of three types—
- It can begin with an incomplete statement followed by several possible endings. You are to find the one ending which *best* completes the statement, although some of the others may not be entirely wrong.
- It can also be a complete statement in the form of a question which is answered by choosing one of the statements listed.

- It can be in the form of a problem – again you select the best answer.

Here is an example of a multiple-choice question with a discussion which should give you some clues as to the method for choosing the right answer:

When an employee has a complaint about his assignment, the action which will *best* help him overcome his difficulty is to
    A. discuss his difficulty with his coworkers
    B. take the problem to the head of the organization
    C. take the problem to the person who gave him the assignment
    D. say nothing to anyone about his complaint

In answering this question, you should study each of the choices to find which is best. Consider choice "A" – Certainly an employee may discuss his complaint with fellow employees, but no change or improvement can result, and the complaint remains unresolved. Choice "B" is a poor choice since the head of the organization probably does not know what assignment you have been given, and taking your problem to him is known as "going over the head" of the supervisor. The supervisor, or person who made the assignment, is the person who can clarify it or correct any injustice. Choice "C" is, therefore, correct. To say nothing, as in choice "D," is unwise. Supervisors have and interest in knowing the problems employees are facing, and the employee is seeking a solution to his problem.

2) True/False Questions

The "true/false" or "right/wrong" form of question is sometimes used. Here a complete statement is given. Your job is to decide whether the statement is right or wrong.

SAMPLE: A roaming cell-phone call to a nearby city costs less than a non-roaming call to a distant city.

This statement is wrong, or false, since roaming calls are more expensive.

This is not a complete list of all possible question forms, although most of the others are variations of these common types. You will always get complete directions for answering questions. Be sure you understand *how* to mark your answers – ask questions until you do.

V. RECORDING YOUR ANSWERS

Computer terminals are used more and more today for many different kinds of exams.

For an examination with very few applicants, you may be told to record your answers in the test booklet itself. Separate answer sheets are much more common. If this separate answer sheet is to be scored by machine – and this is often the case – it is highly important that you mark your answers correctly in order to get credit.

An electronic scoring machine is often used in civil service offices because of the speed with which papers can be scored. Machine-scored answer sheets must be marked with a pencil, which will be given to you. This pencil has a high graphite content which responds to the electronic scoring machine. As a matter of fact, stray dots may register as answers, so do not let your pencil rest on the answer sheet while you are pondering the correct answer. Also, if your pencil lead breaks or is otherwise defective, ask for another.

Since the answer sheet will be dropped in a slot in the scoring machine, be careful not to bend the corners or get the paper crumpled.

The answer sheet normally has five vertical columns of numbers, with 30 numbers to a column. These numbers correspond to the question numbers in your test booklet. After each number, going across the page are four or five pairs of dotted lines. These short dotted lines have small letters or numbers above them. The first two pairs may also have a "T" or "F" above the letters. This indicates that the first two pairs only are to be used if the questions are of the true-false type. If the questions are multiple choice, disregard the "T" and "F" and pay attention only to the small letters or numbers.

Answer your questions in the manner of the sample that follows:

32. The largest city in the United States is
    A. Washington, D.C.
    B. New York City
    C. Chicago
    D. Detroit
    E. San Francisco

1) Choose the answer you think is best. (New York City is the largest, so "B" is correct.)
2) Find the row of dotted lines numbered the same as the question you are answering. (Find row number 32)
3) Find the pair of dotted lines corresponding to the answer. (Find the pair of lines under the mark "B.")
4) Make a solid black mark between the dotted lines.

VI. BEFORE THE TEST

Common sense will help you find procedures to follow to get ready for an examination. Too many of us, however, overlook these sensible measures. Indeed, nervousness and fatigue have been found to be the most serious reasons why applicants fail to do their best on civil service tests. Here is a list of reminders:

- Begin your preparation early – Don't wait until the last minute to go scurrying around for books and materials or to find out what the position is all about.
- Prepare continuously – An hour a night for a week is better than an all-night cram session. This has been definitely established. What is more, a night a week for a month will return better dividends than crowding your study into a shorter period of time.
- Locate the place of the exam – You have been sent a notice telling you when and where to report for the examination. If the location is in a different town or otherwise unfamiliar to you, it would be well to inquire the best route and learn something about the building.
- Relax the night before the test – Allow your mind to rest. Do not study at all that night. Plan some mild recreation or diversion; then go to bed early and get a good night's sleep.
- Get up early enough to make a leisurely trip to the place for the test – This way unforeseen events, traffic snarls, unfamiliar buildings, etc. will not upset you.
- Dress comfortably – A written test is not a fashion show. You will be known by number and not by name, so wear something comfortable.

- Leave excess paraphernalia at home – Shopping bags and odd bundles will get in your way. You need bring only the items mentioned in the official notice you received; usually everything you need is provided. Do not bring reference books to the exam. They will only confuse those last minutes and be taken away from you when in the test room.
- Arrive somewhat ahead of time – If because of transportation schedules you must get there very early, bring a newspaper or magazine to take your mind off yourself while waiting.
- Locate the examination room – When you have found the proper room, you will be directed to the seat or part of the room where you will sit. Sometimes you are given a sheet of instructions to read while you are waiting. Do not fill out any forms until you are told to do so; just read them and be prepared.
- Relax and prepare to listen to the instructions
- If you have any physical problem that may keep you from doing your best, be sure to tell the test administrator. If you are sick or in poor health, you really cannot do your best on the exam. You can come back and take the test some other time.

VII. AT THE TEST

The day of the test is here and you have the test booklet in your hand. The temptation to get going is very strong. Caution! There is more to success than knowing the right answers. You must know how to identify your papers and understand variations in the type of short-answer question used in this particular examination. Follow these suggestions for maximum results from your efforts:

1) Cooperate with the monitor

The test administrator has a duty to create a situation in which you can be as much at ease as possible. He will give instructions, tell you when to begin, check to see that you are marking your answer sheet correctly, and so on. He is not there to guard you, although he will see that your competitors do not take unfair advantage. He wants to help you do your best.

2) Listen to all instructions

Don't jump the gun! Wait until you understand all directions. In most civil service tests you get more time than you need to answer the questions. So don't be in a hurry. Read each word of instructions until you clearly understand the meaning. Study the examples, listen to all announcements and follow directions. Ask questions if you do not understand what to do.

3) Identify your papers

Civil service exams are usually identified by number only. You will be assigned a number; you must not put your name on your test papers. Be sure to copy your number correctly. Since more than one exam may be given, copy your exact examination title.

4) Plan your time

Unless you are told that a test is a "speed" or "rate of work" test, speed itself is usually not important. Time enough to answer all the questions will be provided, but this does not mean that you have all day. An overall time limit has been set. Divide the total time (in minutes) by the number of questions to determine the approximate time you have for each question.

5) Do not linger over difficult questions

If you come across a difficult question, mark it with a paper clip (useful to have along) and come back to it when you have been through the booklet. One caution if you do this – be sure to skip a number on your answer sheet as well. Check often to be sure that you have not lost your place and that you are marking in the row numbered the same as the question you are answering.

6) Read the questions

Be sure you know what the question asks! Many capable people are unsuccessful because they failed to *read* the questions correctly.

7) Answer all questions

Unless you have been instructed that a penalty will be deducted for incorrect answers, it is better to guess than to omit a question.

8) Speed tests

It is often better NOT to guess on speed tests. It has been found that on timed tests people are tempted to spend the last few seconds before time is called in marking answers at random – without even reading them – in the hope of picking up a few extra points. To discourage this practice, the instructions may warn you that your score will be "corrected" for guessing. That is, a penalty will be applied. The incorrect answers will be deducted from the correct ones, or some other penalty formula will be used.

9) Review your answers

If you finish before time is called, go back to the questions you guessed or omitted to give them further thought. Review other answers if you have time.

10) Return your test materials

If you are ready to leave before others have finished or time is called, take ALL your materials to the monitor and leave quietly. Never take any test material with you. The monitor can discover whose papers are not complete, and taking a test booklet may be grounds for disqualification.

VIII. EXAMINATION TECHNIQUES

1) Read the general instructions carefully. These are usually printed on the first page of the exam booklet. As a rule, these instructions refer to the timing of the examination; the fact that you should not start work until the signal and must stop work at a signal, etc. If there are any *special* instructions, such as a choice of questions to be answered, make sure that you note this instruction carefully.

2) When you are ready to start work on the examination, that is as soon as the signal has been given, read the instructions to each question booklet, underline any key words or phrases, such as *least, best, outline, describe* and the like. In this way you will tend to answer as requested rather than discover on reviewing your paper that you *listed without describing*, that you selected the *worst* choice rather than the *best* choice, etc.

3) If the examination is of the objective or multiple-choice type – that is, each question will also give a series of possible answers: A, B, C or D, and you are called upon to select the best answer and write the letter next to that answer on your answer paper – it is advisable to start answering each question in turn. There may be anywhere from 50 to 100 such questions in the three or four hours allotted and you can see how much time would be taken if you read through all the questions before beginning to answer any. Furthermore, if you come across a question or group of questions which you know would be difficult to answer, it would undoubtedly affect your handling of all the other questions.

4) If the examination is of the essay type and contains but a few questions, it is a moot point as to whether you should read all the questions before starting to answer any one. Of course, if you are given a choice – say five out of seven and the like – then it is essential to read all the questions so you can eliminate the two that are most difficult. If, however, you are asked to answer all the questions, there may be danger in trying to answer the easiest one first because you may find that you will spend too much time on it. The best technique is to answer the first question, then proceed to the second, etc.

5) Time your answers. Before the exam begins, write down the time it started, then add the time allowed for the examination and write down the time it must be completed, then divide the time available somewhat as follows:
    - If 3-1/2 hours are allowed, that would be 210 minutes. If you have 80 objective-type questions, that would be an average of 2-1/2 minutes per question. Allow yourself no more than 2 minutes per question, or a total of 160 minutes, which will permit about 50 minutes to review.
    - If for the time allotment of 210 minutes there are 7 essay questions to answer, that would average about 30 minutes a question. Give yourself only 25 minutes per question so that you have about 35 minutes to review.

6) The most important instruction is to *read each question* and make sure you know what is wanted. The second most important instruction is to *time yourself properly* so that you answer every question. The third most important instruction is to *answer every question*. Guess if you have to but include something for each question. Remember that you will receive no credit for a blank and will probably receive some credit if you write something in answer to an essay question. If you guess a letter – say "B" for a multiple-choice question – you may have guessed right. If you leave a blank as an answer to a multiple-choice question, the examiners may respect your feelings but it will not add a point to your score. Some exams may penalize you for wrong answers, so in such cases *only*, you may not want to guess unless you have some basis for your answer.

7) Suggestions
   a. Objective-type questions
      1. Examine the question booklet for proper sequence of pages and questions
      2. Read all instructions carefully
      3. Skip any question which seems too difficult; return to it after all other questions have been answered
      4. Apportion your time properly; do not spend too much time on any single question or group of questions

5. Note and underline key words – *all, most, fewest, least, best, worst, same, opposite,* etc.
6. Pay particular attention to negatives
7. Note unusual option, e.g., unduly long, short, complex, different or similar in content to the body of the question
8. Observe the use of "hedging" words – *probably, may, most likely,* etc.
9. Make sure that your answer is put next to the same number as the question
10. Do not second-guess unless you have good reason to believe the second answer is definitely more correct
11. Cross out original answer if you decide another answer is more accurate; do not erase until you are ready to hand your paper in
12. Answer all questions; guess unless instructed otherwise
13. Leave time for review

b. Essay questions
1. Read each question carefully
2. Determine exactly what is wanted. Underline key words or phrases.
3. Decide on outline or paragraph answer
4. Include many different points and elements unless asked to develop any one or two points or elements
5. Show impartiality by giving pros and cons unless directed to select one side only
6. Make and write down any assumptions you find necessary to answer the questions
7. Watch your English, grammar, punctuation and choice of words
8. Time your answers; don't crowd material

8) Answering the essay question

Most essay questions can be answered by framing the specific response around several key words or ideas. Here are a few such key words or ideas:

M's: manpower, materials, methods, money, management
P's: purpose, program, policy, plan, procedure, practice, problems, pitfalls, personnel, public relations

a. Six basic steps in handling problems:
1. Preliminary plan and background development
2. Collect information, data and facts
3. Analyze and interpret information, data and facts
4. Analyze and develop solutions as well as make recommendations
5. Prepare report and sell recommendations
6. Install recommendations and follow up effectiveness

b. Pitfalls to avoid
1. *Taking things for granted* – A statement of the situation does not necessarily imply that each of the elements is necessarily true; for example, a complaint may be invalid and biased so that all that can be taken for granted is that a complaint has been registered

2. *Considering only one side of a situation* – Wherever possible, indicate several alternatives and then point out the reasons you selected the best one
3. *Failing to indicate follow up* – Whenever your answer indicates action on your part, make certain that you will take proper follow-up action to see how successful your recommendations, procedures or actions turn out to be
4. *Taking too long in answering any single question* – Remember to time your answers properly

IX. AFTER THE TEST

Scoring procedures differ in detail among civil service jurisdictions although the general principles are the same. Whether the papers are hand-scored or graded by machine we have described, they are nearly always graded by number. That is, the person who marks the paper knows only the number – never the name – of the applicant. Not until all the papers have been graded will they be matched with names. If other tests, such as training and experience or oral interview ratings have been given, scores will be combined. Different parts of the examination usually have different weights. For example, the written test might count 60 percent of the final grade, and a rating of training and experience 40 percent. In many jurisdictions, veterans will have a certain number of points added to their grades.

After the final grade has been determined, the names are placed in grade order and an eligible list is established. There are various methods for resolving ties between those who get the same final grade – probably the most common is to place first the name of the person whose application was received first. Job offers are made from the eligible list in the order the names appear on it. You will be notified of your grade and your rank as soon as all these computations have been made. This will be done as rapidly as possible.

People who are found to meet the requirements in the announcement are called "eligibles." Their names are put on a list of eligible candidates. An eligible's chances of getting a job depend on how high he stands on this list and how fast agencies are filling jobs from the list.

When a job is to be filled from a list of eligibles, the agency asks for the names of people on the list of eligibles for that job. When the civil service commission receives this request, it sends to the agency the names of the three people highest on this list. Or, if the job to be filled has specialized requirements, the office sends the agency the names of the top three persons who meet these requirements from the general list.

The appointing officer makes a choice from among the three people whose names were sent to him. If the selected person accepts the appointment, the names of the others are put back on the list to be considered for future openings.

That is the rule in hiring from all kinds of eligible lists, whether they are for typist, carpenter, chemist, or something else. For every vacancy, the appointing officer has his choice of any one of the top three eligibles on the list. This explains why the person whose name is on top of the list sometimes does not get an appointment when some of the persons lower on the list do. If the appointing officer chooses the second or third eligible, the No. 1 eligible does not get a job at once, but stays on the list until he is appointed or the list is terminated.

X. HOW TO PASS THE INTERVIEW TEST

The examination for which you applied requires an oral interview test. You have already taken the written test and you are now being called for the interview test – the final part of the formal examination.

You may think that it is not possible to prepare for an interview test and that there are no procedures to follow during an interview. Our purpose is to point out some things you can do in advance that will help you and some good rules to follow and pitfalls to avoid while you are being interviewed.

What is an interview supposed to test?

The written examination is designed to test the technical knowledge and competence of the candidate; the oral is designed to evaluate intangible qualities, not readily measured otherwise, and to establish a list showing the relative fitness of each candidate – as measured against his competitors – for the position sought. Scoring is not on the basis of "right" and "wrong," but on a sliding scale of values ranging from "not passable" to "outstanding." As a matter of fact, it is possible to achieve a relatively low score without a single "incorrect" answer because of evident weakness in the qualities being measured.

Occasionally, an examination may consist entirely of an oral test – either an individual or a group oral. In such cases, information is sought concerning the technical knowledges and abilities of the candidate, since there has been no written examination for this purpose. More commonly, however, an oral test is used to supplement a written examination.

Who conducts interviews?

The composition of oral boards varies among different jurisdictions. In nearly all, a representative of the personnel department serves as chairman. One of the members of the board may be a representative of the department in which the candidate would work. In some cases, "outside experts" are used, and, frequently, a businessman or some other representative of the general public is asked to serve. Labor and management or other special groups may be represented. The aim is to secure the services of experts in the appropriate field.

However the board is composed, it is a good idea (and not at all improper or unethical) to ascertain in advance of the interview who the members are and what groups they represent. When you are introduced to them, you will have some idea of their backgrounds and interests, and at least you will not stutter and stammer over their names.

What should be done before the interview?

While knowledge about the board members is useful and takes some of the surprise element out of the interview, there is other preparation which is more substantive. It *is* possible to prepare for an oral interview – in several ways:

1) Keep a copy of your application and review it carefully before the interview

This may be the only document before the oral board, and the starting point of the interview. Know what education and experience you have listed there, and the sequence and dates of all of it. Sometimes the board will ask you to review the highlights of your experience for them; you should not have to hem and haw doing it.

2) Study the class specification and the examination announcement

Usually, the oral board has one or both of these to guide them. The qualities, characteristics or knowledges required by the position sought are stated in these documents. They offer valuable clues as to the nature of the oral interview. For example, if the job involves supervisory responsibilities, the announcement will usually indicate that knowledge of modern supervisory methods and the qualifications of the candidate as a supervisor will be tested. If so, you can expect such questions, frequently in the form of a hypothetical situation which you are expected to solve. NEVER go into an oral without knowledge of the duties and responsibilities of the job you seek.

3) Think through each qualification required

Try to visualize the kind of questions you would ask if you were a board member. How well could you answer them? Try especially to appraise your own knowledge and background in each area, *measured against the job sought*, and identify any areas in which you are weak. Be critical and realistic – do not flatter yourself.

4) Do some general reading in areas in which you feel you may be weak

For example, if the job involves supervision and your past experience has NOT, some general reading in supervisory methods and practices, particularly in the field of human relations, might be useful. Do NOT study agency procedures or detailed manuals. The oral board will be testing your understanding and capacity, not your memory.

5) Get a good night's sleep and watch your general health and mental attitude

You will want a clear head at the interview. Take care of a cold or any other minor ailment, and of course, no hangovers.

What should be done on the day of the interview?

Now comes the day of the interview itself. Give yourself plenty of time to get there. Plan to arrive somewhat ahead of the scheduled time, particularly if your appointment is in the fore part of the day. If a previous candidate fails to appear, the board might be ready for you a bit early. By early afternoon an oral board is almost invariably behind schedule if there are many candidates, and you may have to wait. Take along a book or magazine to read, or your application to review, but leave any extraneous material in the waiting room when you go in for your interview. In any event, relax and compose yourself.

The matter of dress is important. The board is forming impressions about you – from your experience, your manners, your attitude, and your appearance. Give your personal appearance careful attention. Dress your best, but not your flashiest. Choose conservative, appropriate clothing, and be sure it is immaculate. This is a business interview, and your appearance should indicate that you regard it as such. Besides, being well groomed and properly dressed will help boost your confidence.

Sooner or later, someone will call your name and escort you into the interview room. *This is it.* From here on you are on your own. It is too late for any more preparation. But remember, you asked for this opportunity to prove your fitness, and you are here because your request was granted.

What happens when you go in?

The usual sequence of events will be as follows: The clerk (who is often the board stenographer) will introduce you to the chairman of the oral board, who will introduce you to the other members of the board. Acknowledge the introductions before you sit down. Do not be surprised if you find a microphone facing you or a stenotypist sitting by. Oral interviews are usually recorded in the event of an appeal or other review.

Usually the chairman of the board will open the interview by reviewing the highlights of your education and work experience from your application – primarily for the benefit of the other members of the board, as well as to get the material into the record. Do not interrupt or comment unless there is an error or significant misinterpretation; if that is the case, do not hesitate. But do not quibble about insignificant matters. Also, he will usually ask you some question about your education, experience or your present job – partly to get you to start talking and to establish the interviewing "rapport." He may start the actual questioning, or turn it over to one of the other members. Frequently, each member undertakes the questioning on a particular area, one in which he is perhaps most competent, so you can expect each member to participate in the examination. Because time is limited, you may also expect some rather abrupt switches in the direction the questioning takes, so do not be upset by it. Normally, a board member will not pursue a single line of questioning unless he discovers a particular strength or weakness.

After each member has participated, the chairman will usually ask whether any member has any further questions, then will ask you if you have anything you wish to add. Unless you are expecting this question, it may floor you. Worse, it may start you off on an extended, extemporaneous speech. The board is not usually seeking more information. The question is principally to offer you a last opportunity to present further qualifications or to indicate that you have nothing to add. So, if you feel that a significant qualification or characteristic has been overlooked, it is proper to point it out in a sentence or so. Do not compliment the board on the thoroughness of their examination – they have been sketchy, and you know it. If you wish, merely say, "No thank you, I have nothing further to add." This is a point where you can "talk yourself out" of a good impression or fail to present an important bit of information. Remember, *you close the interview yourself.*

The chairman will then say, "That is all, Mr. _____, thank you." Do not be startled; the interview is over, and quicker than you think. Thank him, gather your belongings and take your leave. Save your sigh of relief for the other side of the door.

How to put your best foot forward

Throughout this entire process, you may feel that the board individually and collectively is trying to pierce your defenses, seek out your hidden weaknesses and embarrass and confuse you. Actually, this is not true. They are obliged to make an appraisal of your qualifications for the job you are seeking, and they want to see you in your best light. Remember, they must interview all candidates and a non-cooperative candidate may become a failure in spite of their best efforts to bring out his qualifications. Here are 15 suggestions that will help you:

1) Be natural – Keep your attitude confident, not cocky

If you are not confident that you can do the job, do not expect the board to be. Do not apologize for your weaknesses, try to bring out your strong points. The board is interested in a positive, not negative, presentation. Cockiness will antagonize any board member and make him wonder if you are covering up a weakness by a false show of strength.

2) Get comfortable, but don't lounge or sprawl

Sit erectly but not stiffly. A careless posture may lead the board to conclude that you are careless in other things, or at least that you are not impressed by the importance of the occasion. Either conclusion is natural, even if incorrect. Do not fuss with your clothing, a pencil or an ashtray. Your hands may occasionally be useful to emphasize a point; do not let them become a point of distraction.

3) Do not wisecrack or make small talk

This is a serious situation, and your attitude should show that you consider it as such. Further, the time of the board is limited – they do not want to waste it, and neither should you.

4) Do not exaggerate your experience or abilities
   In the first place, from information in the application or other interviews and sources, the board may know more about you than you think. Secondly, you probably will not get away with it. An experienced board is rather adept at spotting such a situation, so do not take the chance.

5) If you know a board member, do not make a point of it, yet do not hide it
   Certainly you are not fooling him, and probably not the other members of the board. Do not try to take advantage of your acquaintanceship – it will probably do you little good.

6) Do not dominate the interview
   Let the board do that. They will give you the clues – do not assume that you have to do all the talking. Realize that the board has a number of questions to ask you, and do not try to take up all the interview time by showing off your extensive knowledge of the answer to the first one.

7) Be attentive
   You only have 20 minutes or so, and you should keep your attention at its sharpest throughout. When a member is addressing a problem or question to you, give him your undivided attention. Address your reply principally to him, but do not exclude the other board members.

8) Do not interrupt
   A board member may be stating a problem for you to analyze. He will ask you a question when the time comes. Let him state the problem, and wait for the question.

9) Make sure you understand the question
   Do not try to answer until you are sure what the question is. If it is not clear, restate it in your own words or ask the board member to clarify it for you. However, do not haggle about minor elements.

10) Reply promptly but not hastily
   A common entry on oral board rating sheets is "candidate responded readily," or "candidate hesitated in replies." Respond as promptly and quickly as you can, but do not jump to a hasty, ill-considered answer.

11) Do not be peremptory in your answers
   A brief answer is proper – but do not fire your answer back. That is a losing game from your point of view. The board member can probably ask questions much faster than you can answer them.

12) Do not try to create the answer you think the board member wants
   He is interested in what kind of mind you have and how it works – not in playing games. Furthermore, he can usually spot this practice and will actually grade you down on it.

13) Do not switch sides in your reply merely to agree with a board member
   Frequently, a member will take a contrary position merely to draw you out and to see if you are willing and able to defend your point of view. Do not start a debate, yet do not surrender a good position. If a position is worth taking, it is worth defending.

14) Do not be afraid to admit an error in judgment if you are shown to be wrong

The board knows that you are forced to reply without any opportunity for careful consideration. Your answer may be demonstrably wrong. If so, admit it and get on with the interview.

15) Do not dwell at length on your present job

The opening question may relate to your present assignment. Answer the question but do not go into an extended discussion. You are being examined for a *new* job, not your present one. As a matter of fact, try to phrase ALL your answers in terms of the job for which you are being examined.

Basis of Rating

Probably you will forget most of these "do's" and "don'ts" when you walk into the oral interview room. Even remembering them all will not ensure you a passing grade. Perhaps you did not have the qualifications in the first place. But remembering them will help you to put your best foot forward, without treading on the toes of the board members.

Rumor and popular opinion to the contrary notwithstanding, an oral board wants you to make the best appearance possible. They know you are under pressure – but they also want to see how you respond to it as a guide to what your reaction would be under the pressures of the job you seek. They will be influenced by the degree of poise you display, the personal traits you show and the manner in which you respond.

ABOUT THIS BOOK

This book contains tests divided into Examination Sections. Go through each test, answering every question in the margin. We have also attached a sample answer sheet at the back of the book that can be removed and used. At the end of each test look at the answer key and check your answers. On the ones you got wrong, look at the right answer choice and learn. Do not fill in the answers first. Do not memorize the questions and answers, but understand the answer and principles involved. On your test, the questions will likely be different from the samples. Questions are changed and new ones added. If you understand these past questions you should have success with any changes that arise. Tests may consist of several types of questions. We have additional books on each subject should more study be advisable or necessary for you. Finally, the more you study, the better prepared you will be. This book is intended to be the last thing you study before you walk into the examination room. Prior study of relevant texts is also recommended. NLC publishes some of these in our Fundamental Series. Knowledge and good sense are important factors in passing your exam. Good luck also helps. So now study this Passbook, absorb the material contained within and take that knowledge into the examination. Then do your best to pass that exam.

EXAMINATION SECTION

EXAMINATION SECTION
TEST 1

DIRECTIONS: Each question or incomplete statement is followed by several suggested answers or completions. Select the one that BEST answers the question or completes the statement. *PRINT THE LETTER OF IN THE CORRECT ANSWER THE SPACE AT THE RIGHT.*

1. Reports show that more men than women are physically handicapped MAINLY because 1.____

    A. women are instinctively more cautious than men
    B. men are more likely to have congenital deformities
    C. women tend to seek surgical remedies because of greater concern over personal appearance
    D. men have lower ability to recover from injury
    E. men are more likely to be exposed to hazardous conditions

2. Of the following, the explanation married women give MOST frequently for seeking employment outside the home is that they wish to 2.____

    A. escape the drudgeries of home life
    B. develop secondary employment skills
    C. maintain an emotionally satisfying career
    D. provide the main support for the family
    E. supplement the family income

3. Of the following home conditions, the one *most likely* to cause emotional disturbances in children is 3.____

    A. increased birthrate following the war
    B. disrupted family relationships
    C. lower family income than that of neighbors
    D. higher family income than that of neighbors
    E. overcrowded living conditions

4. Casual unemployment, as distinguished from other types of unemployment, is traceable MOST readily to 4.____

    A. a decrease in the demand for labor as a result of scientific progress
    B. more or less haphazard changes in the demand for labor in certain industries
    C. periodic changes in the demand for labor in certain industries
    D. disturbances and disruptions in industry resulting from international trade barriers
    E. increased mobility of the population

5. Labor legislation, although primarily intended for the benefit of the employee, MAY aid the employer by 5.____

    A. increasing his control over the immediate labor market
    B. prohibiting government interference with operating policies
    C. protecting him, through equalization of labor costs, from being undercut by other employers
    D. transferring to the general taxpayer the principal costs of industrial hazards of accident and unemployment
    E. increasing the pensions of civil service employees

6. When employment and unemployment figures both decline, the MOST probable conclusion is that

   A. the population has reached a condition of equilibrium
   B. seasonal employment has ended
   C. the labor force has decreased
   D. payments for unemployment insurance have been increased
   E. industrial progress has reduced working hours

7. An individual with an I.Q. of 100 may be said to have demonstrated _____ intelligence.

   A. superior
   B. absolute
   C. substandard
   D. approximately average
   E. high average

8. While state legislatures differ in many respects, all of them are *most nearly* alike in

   A. provisions for retirement of members
   B. rate of pay
   C. length of legislative sessions
   D. method of selection of their members
   E. length of term of office

9. If a state passed a law in a field under Congressional jurisdiction and if Congress subsequently passed contrary legislation, the state provision would be

   A. regarded as never having existed
   B. valid until the next session of the state legislature, which would be obliged to repeal it
   C. superseded by the federal statute
   D. ratified by Congress
   E. still operative in the state involved

10. Power to pardon offenses committed against the people of the United States is vested in the

    A. Supreme Court of the United States
    B. United States District Courts
    C. Federal Bureau of Investigation
    D. United States Parole Board
    E. President of the United States

11. As distinguished from formal social control of an individual's behavior, an example of informal social control is that exerted by

    A. public opinion
    B. religious doctrine
    C. educational institutions
    D. statutes
    E. public health measures

12. The PRINCIPAL function of the jury in a jury trial is to decide questions of

    A. equity
    B. fact
    C. injunction
    D. contract
    E. law

13. Of the following rights of an individual, the one which usually depends on citizenship as distinguished from those given anyone living under the laws of the United States is the right to

    A. receive public assistance
    B. hold an elective office
    C. petition the government for redress of grievances
    D. receive equal protection of the laws
    E. be accorded a trial by jury

14. If the characteristics of a person were being studied by competent observers, it would be expected that their observations would differ MOST markedly with respect to their evaluation of the person's

    A. intelligence
    B. nutritional condition
    C. temperamental characteristics
    D. weight
    E. height

15. If there are evidences of dietary deficiency in families where cereals make up a major portion of the diet, the *most likely* reason for this deficiency is that

    A. cereals cause absorption of excessive quantities of water
    B. persons who concentrate their diet on cereals do not chew their food properly
    C. carbohydrates are deleterious
    D. other essential food elements are omitted
    E. children eat cereals too rapidly

16. Although malnutrition is generally associated with poverty, dietary studies of population groups in the United States reveal that

    A. malnutrition is most often due to a deficiency of nutrients found chiefly in high-cost foods
    B. there has been overemphasis of the casual relationship between poverty and malnutrition
    C. malnutrition is found among people with sufficient money to be well fed
    D. a majority of the population in all income groups is undernourished
    E. malnutrition is not a factor in the incidence of rickets

17. The organization which has as one of its primary functions the mitigation of suffering caused by famine, fire, floods, and other national calamities is the

    A. National Safety Council
    B. Salvation Army
    C. Public Administration Service
    D. American National Red Cross
    E. American Legion

18. The MAIN difference between public welfare and private social agencies is that in public agencies,

    A. case records are open to the public
    B. the granting of assistance cannot be sufficiently flexible to meet the varying needs of individual recipients
    C. only financial assistance may be provided
    D. all policies and procedures must be based upon statutory authorizations
    E. economical and efficient administration are stressed because their funds are obtained through public taxation

19. A recipient of relief who is in need of the services of an attorney but is unable to pay the customary fees, should *generally* be referred to the

    A. Small Claims Court
    B. Domestic Relations Court
    C. County Lawyers Association
    D. City Law Department
    E. Legal Aid Society

20. An injured workman should file his claim for workmen's compensation with the

    A. State Labor Relations Board
    B. Division of Placement and Unemployment Insurance
    C. State Industrial Commission
    D. Workmen's Compensation Board
    E. State Insurance Board

21. The type of insurance found MOST frequently among families such as those assisted by the Department of Social Services is

    A. accident
    B. straight life
    C. endowment
    D. industrial
    E. personal liability

22. Of the following items in the standard budget of the Department of Social Services, the one for which actual expenditures would be MOST constant throughout the year is

    A. fuel
    B. housing
    C. medical care
    D. clothing
    E. household replacements

23. The MOST frequent cause of "broken homes" is attributed to the

    A. temperamental incompatibilities of parents and in-laws
    B. extension of the system of children's courts
    C. psychopathic irresponsibility of the parents
    D. institutionalization of one of the spouses
    E. death of one or both spouses

24. In rearing children, the problems of the widower are usually greater than those of the widow, largely because of the   24._____

    A. tendency of widowers to impose excessively rigid moral standards
    B. increased economic hardship
    C. added difficulty of maintaining a desirable home
    D. possibility that a stepmother will be added to the household
    E. prevalent masculine prejudice against pursuits which are inherently feminine

25. Foster-home placement of children is often advocated in preference to institutionalization *primarily* because   25._____

    A. the law does not provide for local supervision of children's institutions
    B. institutions furnish a more expensive type of care
    C. the number of institutions is insufficient compared to the number of children needing care
    D. children are not well treated in institutions
    E. foster homes provide a more normal environment for children

KEY (CORRECT ANSWERS)

1.	E	11.	A
2.	E	12.	B
3.	B	13.	B
4.	B	14.	C
5.	C	15.	D
6.	C	16.	C
7.	D	17.	D
8.	D	18.	D
9.	C	19.	E
10.	E	20.	D

21.	D
22.	B
23.	E
24.	C
25.	E

TEST 2

DIRECTIONS: Each question or incomplete statement is followed by several suggested answers or completions. Select the one that BEST answers the question or completes the statement. *PRINT THE LETTER OF THE CORRECT ANSWER IN THE SPACE AT THE RIGHT.*

1. Of the following, the category MOST likely to yield the greatest reduction in cost to the taxpayer under improved employment conditions is   1.____

    A. home relief, including aid to the homeless
    B. aid to the blind
    C. aid to dependent children
    D. old-age assistance

2. One of the MOST common characteristics of the chronic alcoholic is   2.____

    A. low intelligence level B. wanderlust
    C. psychosis D. egocentricity

3. Of the following factors leading toward the cure of the alcoholic, the MOST important is thought to be   3.____

    A. removal of all alcohol from the immediate environment
    B. development of a sense of personal adequacy
    C. social disapproval of drinking
    D. segregation from former companions

4. The Federal Housing Administration is the agency which   4.____

    A. insures mortgages made by lending institutions for new construction or remodeling of old construction
    B. provides federal aid for state and local government for slum clearance and housing for very low income families
    C. subsidizes the building industry through direct grants
    D. provides for the construction of low-cost housing projects owned and operated by the federal government

5. In comparing the advantages of foster home over institutional placement, it is generally agreed that institutional care is LEAST advisable for children   5.____

    A. who cannot sustain the intimacy of foster family living because of their experiences with their own parents
    B. who are socially well-adjusted or have had considerable experience in living with a family
    C. who have need for special facilities for observation, diagnosis, and treatment
    D. whose natural parents find it difficult to accept the idea of foster home placement because of its close resemblance to adoption

6. The school can play a vital part in detecting the child who displays overt symptomatic behavior indicative of social maladjustment CHIEFLY because the teacher has the opportunity to

    A. assume a pseudo-parental role in regard to discipline and punishment, thereby limiting the extent of the maladjusted child's anti-social behavior
    B. observe how the child relates to the group and what reactions are stimulated in him by his peer relationships
    C. determine whether the adjustment difficulties displayed by the child were brought on by the teacher herself or by the other students
    D. help the child's parents to resolve the difficulties in adjustment which are indicated by the child's reactions to the social pressures exerted by his peers

7. In treating juvenile delinquents, it has been found that there are some who make better social adjustment through group treatment than through an individual casework approach.
   In selecting delinquent boys for group treatment, the one of the following which is the MOST important consideration is that

    A. the boys to be treated in one group be friends or from the same community
    B. only boys who consent to group treatment be included in the group
    C. the ages of the boys included in the group vary as much as possible
    D. only boys who have not reacted to an individual casework approach be included in the group

8. Multi-problem families are generally characterized by various functional indicators.
   Of the following, the family which is *most likely* to be a multi-problem family is one which has

    A. unemployed adult family members
    B. parents with diagnosed character disorders
    C. children and parents with a series of difficulties in the community
    D. poor housekeeping standards

9. Multi-problem families generally have a complex history of intervention by a variety of social agencies.
   Of the following phases involved in planning for their treatment, the one which is MOST important to consider FIRST is the

    A. joint decision to limit any help to be given
    B. analysis of facts and definition of the problems involved
    C. determination of treatment priorities
    D. study of available community resources

10. The development of good public relations in the area for which the supervisor is responsible should be considered by the supervisor as

    A. not his responsibility as he is primarily responsible for his workers' services
    B. dependent upon him as he is in the best position to interpret the department to the community
    C. not important to the adequate functioning of the department
    D. a part of his method of carrying out his job responsibility as what his workers do affects the community

11. Of the following, the LEAST accurate statement concerning the relationship of public and private social agencies is that

    A. both have an important and necessary function to perform
    B. they are not to be considered as competing or rival agencies
    C. they are cooperating agencies
    D. their work is based on fundamentally different social work concepts

12. Of the following, the LEAST accurate statement concerning the worker-client relationship is that the worker should have the ability to

    A. express warmth of feeling in appropriate ways as a basis for a professional relationship which creates confidence
    B. feel appropriately in the relationship without losing the ability to see the situation in the perspective necessary to help the people immersed in it
    C. identify himself with the client so that the worker's personality does not influence the client
    D. use keen observation and perceive what is significant with a new range of appreciation of the meaning of the situation to the client

13. Of the following, the MOST fundamental psychological concept underlying case work in the public assistance field is that

    A. eligibility for public assistance should be reviewed from time to time
    B. workers should be aware of the prevalence of psychological disabilities among members of families on public assistance
    C. workers should realize the necessity of carrying out the policies laid down by the state office in order that state aid may be received
    D. in the process of receiving assistance, recipients should not be deprived of their normal status of self-direction

14. Of the following, the MOST comprehensive as well as the MOST accurate statement concerning the professional attitude of the social worker is that he should

    A. have a real concern for, and an intelligent interest in, the welfare of the client
    B. recognize that the client's feelings rather than the realities of his needs are of major importance to the client
    C. put at the client's service the worker's knowledge and sincere interest in him
    D. use his insight and understanding to make sound decisions about the client

15. The one of the following reasons for refusing a job which is LEAST acceptable, from the viewpoint of maintaining a client's continued rights to unemployment insurance benefits, is that

    A. acceptance of the job would interfere with the client's joining or retaining membership in a labor union
    B. there is a strike, lockout, or other industrial controversy in the establishment where employment is offered
    C. the distance from the place of employment to his home is greater than seems justified to the client
    D. the wages offered are lower than the prevailing wages in that locality

15.____

16. Experience pragmatically suggests that dislocation from cultural roots and customs makes for tension, insecurity, and anxiety. This holds for the child as well as the adolescent, for the new immigrant as well as the second-generation citizen.
Of the following, the MOST important implication of the above statement for a social worker in any setting is that

    A. anxiety, distress, and incapacity are always personal and can be understood best only through an understanding of the child's present cultural environment
    B. in order to resolve the conflicts caused by the displacement of a child from a home with one cultural background to one with another, it is essential that the child fully replace his old culture with the new one
    C. no treatment goal can be envisaged for a dislocated child which does not involve a value judgment which is itself culturally determined
    D. anxiety and distress result from a child's reaction to culturally oriented treatment goals

16.____

17. Accepting the fact that mentally gifted children represent superior heredity, the United States faces an important eugenic problem CHIEFLY because

    A. unless these mentally gifted children mature and reproduce more rapidly than the less intelligent children, the nation is heading for a lowering of the average intelligence of its people
    B. although the mentally gifted child always excels scholastically, he generally has less physical stamina than the normal child and tends to lower the nation's population physically
    C. the mentally subnormal are increasing more rapidly than the mentally gifted in America, thus affecting the overall level of achievement of the gifted child
    D. unless the mental level of the general population is raised to that of the gifted child, the mentally gifted will eventually usurp the reigns of government and dominate the mentally weaker

17.____

18. The form of psychiatric treatment which requires the LEAST amount of participation on the part of the patient is

    A. psychoanalysis   B. psychotherapy
    C. shock therapy   D. non-directive therapy

18.____

19. Tests administered by psychologists for the PRIMARY purpose of measuring intelligence are known as _____ tests.

   A. projective
   B. validating
   C. psychometric
   D. apperception

20. In recent years, there have been some significant changes in the treatment of patients in state psychiatric hospitals. These changes are PRIMARILY caused by the use of

   A. electric shock therapy
   B. tranquilizing drugs
   C. steroids
   D. the open-ward policy

21. The psychological test which makes use of a set of twenty pictures, each depicting a dramatic scene, is known as the

   A. Goodenough Test
   B. Thematic Apperception Test
   C. Minnesota Multiphasic Personality Inventory
   D. Healy Picture Completion Test

22. One of the MOST effective ways in which experimental psychologists have been able to study the effects on personality of heredity and environment has been through the study of

   A. primitive cultures
   B. identical twins
   C. mental defectives
   D. newborn infants

23. In hospitals with psychiatric divisions, the psychiatric function is PREDOMINANTLY that of

   A. the training of personnel in all psychiatric disciplines
   B. protection of the community against potentially dangerous psychiatric patients
   C. research and study of psychiatric patients so that new knowledge and information can be made generally available
   D. short-term hospitalization designed to determine diagnosis and recommendations for treatment

24. Predictions of human behavior on the basis of past behavior frequently are INACCURATE because

   A. basic patterns of human behavior are in a continual state of flux
   B. human behavior is not susceptible to explanation of a scientific nature
   C. the underlying psychological mechanisms of behavior are not completely understood
   D. quantitative techniques for the measurement of stimuli and responses are unavailable

25. Socio-cultural factors are being re-evaluated in casework practice as they influence both the worker and the client in their participation in the casework process.
Of the following factors, the one which is currently being studied MOST widely is the

    A. social class of worker and client and its significance in casework
    B. difference in native intelligence which can be ascribed to racial origin of an individual
    C. cultural values affecting the areas in which an individual functions
    D. necessity in casework treatment of the client's membership in an organized religious group

25.____

KEY (CORRECT ANSWERS)

1.	A	11.	D
2.	D	12.	C
3.	B	13.	D
4.	A	14.	C
5.	B	15.	C
6.	B	16.	C
7.	B	17.	A
8.	C	18.	C
9.	B	19.	C
10.	D	20.	B

21.	B
22.	B
23.	D
24.	C
25.	C

EXAMINATION SECTION
TEST 1

DIRECTIONS: Each question or incomplete statement is followed by several suggested answers or completions. Select the one that BEST answers the question or completes the statement. *PRINT THE LETTER OF THE CORRECT ANSWER IN THE SPACE AT THE RIGHT.*

1. Deviant behavior is a sociological term used to describe behavior which is not in accord with generally accepted standards. This may include juvenile delinquency, adult criminality, mental or physical illness.
Comparison of normal with deviant behavior is useful to social workers because it

    A. makes it possible to establish watertight behavioral descriptions
    B. provides evidence of differential social behavior which distinguishes deviant from normal behavior
    C. indicates that deviant behavior is of no concern to social workers
    D. provides no evidence that social role is a determinant of behavior

1.____

2. Alcoholism may affect an individual client's ability to function as a spouse, parent, worker, and citizen.
A social worker's MAIN responsibility to a client with a history of alcoholism is to

    A. interpret to the client the causes of alcoholism as a disease syndrome
    B. work with the alcoholic's family to accept him as he is and stop trying to reform him
    C. encourage the family of the alcoholic to accept casework treatment
    D. determine the origins of his particular drinking problem, establish a diagnosis, and work out a treatment plan for him

2.____

3. There is a trend to regard narcotic addiction as a form of illness for which the current methods of intervention have not been effective.
Research on the combination of social, psychological, and physical causes of addiction would indicate that social workers should

    A. oppose hospitalization of addicts in institutions
    B. encourage the addict to live normally at home
    C. recognize that there is no successful treatment for addiction and act accordingly
    D. use the existing community facilities differentially for each addict

3.____

4. A study of social relationships among delinquent and non-delinquent youth has shown that

    A. delinquent youth generally conceal their true feelings and maintain furtive social contacts
    B. delinquents are more impulsive and vivacious than law-abiding boys
    C. non-delinquent youths diminish their active social relationships in order to sublimate any anti-social impulses
    D. delinquent and non-delinquent youths exhibit similar characteristics of impulsiveness and vivaciousness

4.____

5. The one of the following which is the CHIEF danger of interpreting the delinquent behavior of a child in terms of morality *alone* when attempting to get at its causes is that

   A. this tends to overlook the likelihood that the causes of the child's actions are more than a negation of morality and involve varied symptoms of disturbance
   B. a child's moral outlook toward life and society is largely colored by that of his parents, thus encouraging parent-child conflict
   C. too careful a consideration of the moral aspects of the offense and of the child's needs may often negate the demands of justice in a case
   D. standards of morality may be of no concern to the delinquent and he may not realize the seriousness of his offenses

6. Experts in the field of personnel administration are generally agreed that an employee should not be under the immediate supervision of more than one supervisor. A certain worker, because of an emergency situation, divides his time equally between two limited caseloads on a prearranged time schedule. Each unit has a different supervisor, and the worker performs substantially the same duties in each caseload.
The above statement is pertinent in this situation CHIEFLY because

   A. each supervisor, feeling that the cases in her unit should have priority, may demand too much of the worker's time
   B. the two supervisors may have different standards of work performance and may prefer different methods of doing the work
   C. the worker works part-time on each caseload and may not have full knowledge or control of the situation in either caseload
   D. the task of evaluating the worker's services will be doubled, with two supervisors instead of one having to rate his work

7. Experts in modern personnel management generally agree that employees on all job levels should be permitted to offer suggestions for improving work methods.
Of the following, the CHIEF limitation of such suggestions is that they may, at times,

   A. be offered primarily for financial reward and not show genuine interest in improvement of work methods
   B. be directed towards making individual jobs easier
   C. be restricted by the employees' fear of radically changing the work methods favored by their supervisors
   D. show little awareness of the effects on the overall objectives and functions of the entire agency

8. Through the supervisory process and relationship, the supervisor is trying to help workers gain increased self-awareness.
Of the following statements concerning this process, the one which is MOST accurate is:

   A. Self-awareness is developed gradually so that worker can learn to control his own reactions.
   B. Worker is expected to be introspective primarily for his own enlightenment.
   C. Supervisor is trying to help worker handle any emotional difficulties he may reveal.
   D. Worker is expected at the onset to share and determine with the supervisor what in his previous background makes it difficult for him to use certain ideas.

9. The one of the following statements concerning principles in the learning process which is LEAST accurate is:

   A. Some degree of regression on the part of the worker is usually natural in the process of development and this should be accepted by the supervisor.
   B. When a beginning worker shows problems, the supervisor should first handle this behavior as a personality difficulty.
   C. It has been found in the work training process that some degree of resistance is usually inevitable.
   D. The emotional content of work practice may tend to set up *blind spots* in workers.

10. Of the following, the one that represents the BEST basis for planning the content of a successful staff development program is the

    A. time available for meetings
    B. chief social problems of the community
    C. common needs of the staff workers as related to the situations with which they are dealing
    D. experimental programs conducted by other agencies

11. In planning staff development seminars, the MOST valuable topics for discussion are likely to be those selected from

    A. staff suggestions based on the staff's interest and needs
    B. topics recommended for consideration by professional organizations
    C. topics selected by the administration based on demonstrated limitations of staff skill and knowledge
    D. topics selected by the administration based on a combination of staff interest and objectivity evaluated staff needs

12. Staff meetings designed to promote professional staff development are MOST likely to achieve this goal when

    A. there is the widest participation among all staff members who attend the meetings
    B. participation by the most skilled and experienced staff members is predominant
    C. participation by selected staff members is planned before the meeting sessions
    D. supervisory personnel take major responsibility for participation

13. Assume that you are the leader of a conference attended by representatives of various city and private agencies. After the conference has been underway for a considerable time, you realize that the representative of one of these agencies has said nothing. It would generally be BEST for you to

    A. ask him if he would like to say anything
    B. ask the group a pertinent question that he would probably be best able to answer
    C. make no special effort to include him in the conversation
    D. address the next question you planned to ask to him directly

14. A member of a decision-making conference generally makes his BEST contribution to the conference when he

    A. compromises on his own point of view and accepts most of the points of other conference members
    B. persuades the conference to accept all or most of his points

4 (#1)

C. persuades the conference to accept his major proposals but will yield on the minor ones
D. succeeds in integrating his ideas with the ideas of the other conference members

15. Of the following, the LEAST accurate statement concerning the compilation and use of statistics in administration is:

   A. Interpretation of statistics is as necessary as their compilation.
   B. Statistical records of expenditures and services are one of the bases for budget preparation.
   C. Statistics on the quality of services rendered to the community will clearly delineate the human values achieved.
   D. The results achieved from collecting and compiling statistics must be in keeping with the cost and effort required.

16. An important administrative problem is how precisely to define the limits on authority that is delegated to subordinate supervisors.
Such definition of limits of authority SHOULD be

   A. as precise as possible and practicable in all areas
   B. as precise as possible and practicable in all areas of function, but should allow considerable flexibility in the area of personnel management
   C. as precise as possible and practicable in the area of personnel management, but should allow considerable flexibility in the areas of function
   D. in general terms so as to allow considerable flexibility both in the areas of function and in the areas of personnel management

17. The LEAST important of the following reasons why a particular activity should be assigned to a unit which performs activities dissimilar to it is that

   A. close coordination is needed between the particular activity and other activities performed by the unit
   B. it will enhance the reputation and prestige of the unit supervisor
   C. the unit makes frequent use of the results of this particular activity
   D. the unit supervisor has a sound knowledge and understanding of the particular activity

18. The MOST important of the following reasons why the average resident of a deteriorated slum neighborhood resists relocation to an area in the suburbs with better physical accommodations is that he

   A. does not recognize as undesirable the characteristics which are responsible for deterioration of the neighborhood
   B. has some expectation of neighborly assistance in his old home in times of stress and adversity
   C. hopes for better days when he may be able to become a figure of some importance and envy in the old neighborhood
   D. is attuned to the noise of the city and fears the quiet of the suburb

19. From a psychological and sociological point of view, the MOST important of the following dangers to the persons living in an economically depressed area in which the only step taken by governmental and private social agencies to assist these persons is the granting of a dole is that

   A. industry will be reluctant to expand its operations in that area
   B. the dole will encourage additional non-producers to enter the area
   C. the residents of the area will probably have to find their own solution to their problems
   D. their permanent dependency will be fostered

19._____

20. The term *real wages* is GENERALLY used by economists to mean the

   A. amount of take-home pay left after taxes, social security, and other such deductions have been made by the employer
   B. average wage actually earned during a calendar or fiscal year
   C. family income expressed on a per capita basis
   D. wages expressed in terms of its buyer power

20._____

21. It has, at times, been suggested that an effective way to eradicate juvenile delinquency would be to arrest and punish the parents for the criminal actions of their delinquent children.
The one of the following which is the CHIEF defect of this proposal is that

   A. it fails to get at the cause of the delinquent act and tends to further weaken disturbed parent-child relationships
   B. since the criminally inclined child has apparently demonstrated little love or affection for his parent, the child will be unlikely to amend his behavior in order to avoid hurting his parent
   C. the child who commits anti-social acts does so in many cases in order to hurt his parents so that this proposal would not only increase the parents' sorrow, but would also serve as an incentive to more delinquency by the child
   D. the punishment should be limited to the person who commits the illegal action rather than to those who are most interested in his welfare

21._____

22. Surveys which have compared the relative stability of marriages between white persons with marriages between non-white persons in this country have shown that, among Blacks, there is

   A. a significantly higher percentage of spouses absent from the household than among whites
   B. a significantly higher percentage of spouses absent from the household than among whites living in the South, but the opposite is true in the Northeast
   C. a significantly lower percentage of spouses absent from the household than among whites
   D. no significant difference in the percentage of spouses absent from the household when compared with the white population

22._____

23. A phenomenon found in the cultural and recreational patterns of European immigrant families in America is that, generally, the foreign-born adults

   A. as well as their children, tend soon to forget their old-world activities and adopt the cultural and recreational customs of America
   B. as well as their children, tend to retain and continue their old-world cultural and recreational pursuits, and find it equally difficult to adopt those of America
   C. tend soon to drop their old pursuits and adopt the cultural and recreational patterns of America while their children find it somewhat more difficult to make this change
   D. tend to retain and continue their old-world cultural and recreational pursuits while their children tend to rapidly replace these by the games and cultural patterns of America

24. Certain mores of migrant groups are strengthened under the impact of their contact with the native society while other mores are weakened.
   In the case of Puerto Ricans who have come to the city, the effect of such contact upon their traditional family structure has been a

   A. strengthening of the former maternalistic family structure
   B. strengthening of the former paternalistic family structure
   C. weakening of the former maternalistic family structure
   D. weakening of the former paternalistic family structure

25. Administrative reviews and special studies of independent experts, as reported by the Department of Health, Education and Welfare, indicate that the proportion of recipients of public assistance who receive such assistance through *wilful misrepresentation* of the facts is

   A. less than 1% B. about 4%
   C. between 4% and 7% D. between 7% and 10%

KEY (CORRECT ANSWERS)

1. B	11. D
2. D	12. A
3. D	13. B
4. B	14. D
5. A	15. C
6. B	16. A
7. D	17. B
8. A	18. B
9. B	19. D
10. C	20. D

21. A
22. A
23. D
24. D
25. A

TEST 2

DIRECTIONS: Each question or incomplete statement is followed by several suggested answers or completions. Select the one that BEST answers the question or completes the statement. *PRINT THE LETTER OF THE CORRECT ANSWER IN THE SPACE AT THE RIGHT.*

1. In order to meet more adequately the public assistance needs occasioned by sudden changes in the national economy, social service agencies, in general, recommend, as a matter of preference, that

    A. each locality build up reserve funds to care for needy unemployed persons in order to avoid a breakdown of local resources such as occurred during the depression
    B. the federal government assume total responsibility for the administration of public assistance
    C. state settlement laws be strictly enforced so that unemployed workers will be encouraged to move from the emergency industry centers to their former homes
    D. a federal-state-local program of general assistance be established with need as the only eligibility requirement
    E. eligibility requirements be tightened to assure that only legitimately worthy local residents receive the available assistance

1.____

2. The MOST practical method of maintaining income for the majority of aged persons who are no longer able to work, or for the families of those workers who are deceased, is a(n)

    A. comprehensive system of non-categorical assistance on a basis of cash payments
    B. integrated system of public assistance and extensive work relief programs
    C. co-ordinated system of providing care in institutions and foster homes
    D. system of contributory insurance in which a cash benefit is paid as a matter of right
    E. expanded system of diagnostic and treatment centers

2.____

3. With the establishment of insurance and assistance programs under the Social Security Act, many institutional programs for the aged have tended to the greatest extent toward an increased emphasis on providing, of the following types of assistance,

    A. care for the aged by denominational groups
    B. care for children requiring institutional treatment
    C. recreational facilities for the able-bodied aged
    D. training facilities in industrial homework for the aged
    E. care for the chronically ill and infirm aged

3.____

4. Of the following terms, the one which BEST describes the Social Security Act is

    A. enabling legislation
    B. regulatory statute
    C. appropriations act
    D. act of mandamus
    E. provisional enactment

4.____

19

5. Of the following, the term which MOST accurately describes an appropriation is

   A. authority to spend
   B. itemized estimate
   C. *fund* accounting
   D. anticipated expenditure
   E. executive budget

6. When business expansion causes a demand for labor, the worker group which benefits MOST immediately is the group comprising

   A. employed workers
   B. inexperienced workers under 21 years of age
   C. experienced workers 21 to 25 years of age
   D. inexperienced older workers
   E. experienced workers over 40 years of age

7. The MOST important failure in our present system of providing social work services in local communities is the

   A. absence of adequate facilities for treating mental illness
   B. lack of coordination of available data and service in the community
   C. poor quality of the casework services provided by the public agencies
   D. limitations of the probation and parole services
   E. inadequacy of private family welfare services

8. Recent studies of the relationship between incidence of illness and the use of available treatment services among various population groups in the United States show that

   A. while lower-income families use medical services with greater frequency, total expenditures are greater among the upper-income groups
   B. although the average duration of a period of medical care increases with increasing income, the average frequency of obtaining care decreases with increasing income
   C. adequacy of medical service is inversely related to frequency of illness and size of family income
   D. families in the higher-income brackets have a heavier incidence of illness and make greater use of medical services than do those in the lower-income brackets
   E. both as to frequency and duration, the distribution of illness falls equally on all groups, but the use of medical services increases with income

9. The category of disease which most public health departments and authorities usually are NOT equipped to handle *directly* is that of

   A. chronic disease
   B. bronchial disturbances
   C. venereal disease
   D. mosquito-borne diseases
   E. incipient forms of tuberculosis

3 (#2)

10. Recent statistical analyses of the causes of death in the United States indicate that medical science has now reached the stage where it would be preferable to increase its research toward control, among the following, PRINCIPALLY of

    A. accidents
    B. suicides
    C. communicable disease
    D. chronic disease
    E. infant mortality

11. Although the distinction between mental disease and mental deficiency is fairly definite, both these conditions USUALLY represent

    A. diseases of one part or organ of the body rather than of the whole person
    B. an inadequacy existing from birth or shortly afterwards and appearing as a simplicity of intelligence
    C. a deficiency developing later in life and characterized by distortions of attitude and belief
    D. inadequacies in meeting life situations and in conducting one's affairs
    E. somewhat transitory conditions characterized by disturbances of consciousness

12. According to studies made by reliable medical research organizations in the United States, differences among the states in proportion of physicians to population are MOST directly related to the

    A. geographic resources among the states
    B. skill of the physicians
    C. relative proportions of urban and rural people in the population of the states
    D. number of specialists in the ranks of the physicians
    E. health status of the people in the various states

13. One of the MAIN advantages of incorporating a charitable organization is that

    A. gifts or property of a corporation cannot be held in perpetuity
    B. gifts to unincorporated charitable organizations are not deductible from the taxable income
    C. incorporation gives less legal standing or *personality* than an informal partnership
    D. members of a corporation cannot be held liable for debts contracted by the organization
    E. a corporate organization cannot be sued

14. The BASIC principle underlying a social security program is that the government should provide

    A. aid to families that is not dependent on state or local participation
    B. assistance to any worthy family unable to maintain itself independently
    C. protection to individuals against some of the social risks that are inherent in an industrialized society
    D. safeguards against those factors leading to economic depression

15. The activities of state and local public welfare agencies are dependent to a large degree on the public assistance program of the federal government.
The one of the following which the federal government has NOT been successful in achieving within the local agencies is the

   A. broadening of the scope of public assistance administration
   B. expansion of the categorical programs
   C. improvement of the quality of service given to clients
   D. standardization of the administration of general assistance programs

16. Of the following statements, the one which BEST describes the federal government's position, as stated in the Social Security Act, with regard to tests of character or fitness to be administered by local or state welfare departments to prospective clients is that

   A. no tests of character are required but they are not specifically prohibited
   B. if tests of character are used, they must be uniform throughout the state
   C. tests of character are contrary to the philosophy of the federal government and are to be considered illegal
   D. no tests of character are required, and assistance to those states that use them will be withheld

17. An increase in the size of the welfare grant may increase the cost of the welfare program not only in terms of those already on the welfare rolls, but because it may result in an increase in the number of people on the rolls.
The CHIEF reason that an increase in the size of the grant may cause an increase in the number of people on the rolls is that the increased grant may

   A. induce low-salaried wage earners to apply for assistance rather than continue at their menial jobs
   B. make eligible for assistance many people whose resources are just above the previous standard
   C. induce many people to apply for assistance who hesitated to do so because of meagerness of the previous grant
   D. make relatives less willing to contribute because the welfare grant can more adequately cover their dependents' needs

18. One of the MAIN differences between the use of casework methods by a public welfare agency and by a private welfare agency is that the public welfare agency

   A. requires that the applicant be eligible for the services it offers
   B. cannot maintain a non-judgmental attitude toward its clients because of legal requirements
   C. places less emphasis on efforts to change the behavior of its clients
   D. must be more objective in its approach to the client because public funds are involved

19. All definitions of social casework include certain major assumptions.
Of the following, the one which is NOT considered a major assumption is that

   A. the individual and society are interdependent
   B. social forces influence behavior and attitudes, affording opportunity for self-development and contribution to the world in which we live
   C. reconstruction of the total personality and reorganization of the total environment are specific goals
   D. the client is a responsible participant at every step in the solution of his problems

20. In order to provide those services to problem families which will help restore them to a self-maintaining status, it is necessary to FIRST

   A. develop specific plans to meet the individual needs of the problem family
   B. reduce the size of those caseloads composed of multi-problem families
   C. remove them from their environment and provide them with the means of overcoming their dependency
   D. identify the factors causing their dependency and creating problems for them

21. Of the following, the type of service which can provide the client with the MOST enduring help is that service which

   A. provides him with material aid and relieves the stress of his personal problems
   B. assists him to do as much as he can for himself and leaves him free to make his own decisions
   C. directs his efforts towards returning to a self-maintaining status and provides him with desirable goals
   D. gives him the feeling that the agency is interested in him as an individual and stands ready to assist him with his problems

22. Psychiatric interpretation of unconscious motivations can bring childhood conflicts into the framework of adult understanding and open the way for them to be resolved, but the interpretation must come from within the client.
    This statement means MOST NEARLY that

   A. treatment is merely diagnosis in reverse
   B. explaining a client to himself will lead to the resolution of his problems
   C. the client must arrive at an understanding of his problems
   D. unresolved childhood conflicts create problems for the adult

23. A significant factor in the United States economic picture is the state of the labor market. Of the following, the MOST important development affecting the labor market has been

   A. an expansion of the national defense effort creating new plant capacity
   B. the general increase in personal income as a result of an increase in overtime pay in manufacturing industries
   C. the growth of manufacturing as a result of automation
   D. a demand for a large number of jobs resulting from new job applicants as well as from displacement of workers by automation

24. A typical characteristic of the United States population over 65 is that MOST of them

   A. are independent and capable of self-support
   B. live in their own homes but require various supportive services
   C. live in institutions for the aged
   D. require constant medical attention at home or in an institution

25. The one of the following factors which is MOST important in preventing persons 65 years of age and older from getting employment is the

   A. misconceptions by employers of skills and abilities of senior citizens
   B. lack of skill in modern industrial techniques of persons in this age group
   C. social security laws restricting employment of persons in this age group
   D. unwillingness of persons in this age group to continue supporting themselves

KEY (CORRECT ANSWERS)

1.	D	11.	D
2.	D	12.	C
3.	E	13.	D
4.	A	14.	C
5.	A	15.	D
6.	B	16.	A
7.	B	17.	B
8.	C	18.	C
9.	A	19.	C
10.	D	20.	D

21. B
22. C
23. D
24. B
25. A

———

EXAMINATION SECTION

TEST 1

DIRECTIONS: Each question or incomplete statement is followed by several suggested answers or completions. Select the one that BEST answers the question or completes the statement. *PRINT THE LETTER OF THE CORRECT ANSWER IN THE SPACE AT THE RIGHT.*

1. Of the following, the BEST source of trend information pertaining to occupational data is
    A. *The U.S. Industrial Outlook*
    B. *Estimates of Worker Trait Requirements*
    C. *Occupational Outlook Handbook*
    D. *Dictionary of Occupational Titles*

   1._____

2. Of non-white youngsters in the United States who drop out before completing four years of high school, what proportion come from families earning less than $20,000?
    A. 25%
    B. 40%
    C. More than 50%
    D. More than 90%

   2._____

3. Educational attainment has been rising. Median institution years of attainment for persons now holding clerical or sales jobs average
    A. more than 12 years
    B. less than 12 years
    C. more than 10 years
    D. less than 10 years

   3._____

4. Automation and technological development are causing job displacement throughout the economy. Which industry sector has suffered the most severe job losses due to these factors?
    A. Services
    B. Agriculture
    C. Manufacturing
    D. Professional, technical and managerial occupations

   4._____

5. *Choosing a Vocation*: Frank Parsons; *Mind That Found Itself*: _____
    A. Ralph Berdie
    B. Carl Rogers
    C. Mary L. Northway
    D. Clifford Beers

   5._____

25

6. The counselor will find which one of the books below extremely valuable in developing his occupational information program because it contains a complete annotated bibliography of career materials—books, pamphlets, posters, subscription services, etc.?
    A. Forrester, *Occupational Literature*
    B. Roe, *Psychology of Occupations*
    C. Greenleaf, *Occupations and Careers*
    D. Shartle, *Occupational Information*

6._____

7. The proper sequence of the four occupation categories listed below in accordance with the number of people employed in each, proceeding from highest to lowest, is
    A. manufacturing; government; wholesale and retail trade; services
    B. government; manufacturing; services; wholesale and retail trade
    C. services; wholesale and retail trade; manufacturing; government
    D. manufacturing; wholesale and retail trade; government; services

7._____

8. The vocational guidance movement, which is the parent of current guidance programs, was spearheaded by
    A. Frank Parsons
    B. Clifford Beers
    C. John Brewer
    D. Harry Kitson

8._____

9. Among the following occupational categories, the one expected to grow MOST rapidly in the next ten years is that of
    A. sales workers
    B. skilled workers
    C. managers
    D. clerical workers

9._____

10. The largest quantity of occupational information is published by
    A. Science Research Associates
    B. New York Life Insurance Company
    C. Chronicle Guidance Publications
    D. United States Government

10._____

11. The only occupational field – outside of farming – which has declined in actual numbers of employed since the end of World War II has been the field of
    A. printing trades
    B. tool and die machine work
    C. building construction
    D. unskilled jobs

11._____

12. One of the effects of automation and productivity has been to 12._____
    A. increase the education and training requirements of jobs
    B. eliminate many middlemen in trade and service fields
    C. decrease the number of semi-professional jobs
    D. lower the level of earnings in service jobs

13. Which of the following problems presents the MOST serious challenge to 13._____
    the counselor's skill?
    A. Redirecting the goals of the low-ability, high-aspiration students
    B. Redirecting the goals of the high-ability, low-aspiration students
    C. Changing the direction of a student whose goals are at an appropriate level, but wrongly directed
    D. Encouraging a client to investigate a promising field

14. There are a number of excellent resources for assistance in developing 14._____
    units on vocations. The writings of the specialists vary. Which of the
    following authors should you recommend on vocation?
    A. Gerald T. Kowitz
    B. Walter Lifton
    C. Robert Hoppock
    D. Gilbert Wrenn

15. Of the following occupational categories, the one that provides jobs to the 15._____
    largest number of people is
    A. craftsmen, foremen and kindred workers
    B. operatives and kindred workers
    C. professional, technical and kindred workers
    D. clerical and kindred workers

16. The *Dictionary of Occupational Titles* has developed a new coding 16._____
    system. Which of the following categories is NOT part of the code?
    A. Data   B. Ideas   C. People   D. Things

17. The most recent edition of the *Dictionary of Occupational Titles* includes 17._____
    all of the following EXCEPT
    A. the outlook for particular occupations in the next five to ten years
    B. bound volumes of occupational listings and descriptions
    C. occupations likely to be found in any industry
    D. training requirements and methods of entry into occupations

18. Most women who take jobs do so because of 18._____
    A. financial necessity
    B. desire to escape from boredom at home
    C. personal satisfaction
    D. desire to provide some extra luxuries for the home

19. The single largest employer of labor in this nation is which of the following industry divisions?   19._____
    A. Manufacturing
    B. Government
    C. Wholesale and retail trade
    D. Construction

20. High school seniors dropping out before graduation are MOST likely to come from a household where the family head is which one of the following?   20._____
    A. White-collar worker
    B. Manual service worker
    C. Farm worker
    D. Unemployed or not in labor force

21. Of the following, the BEST source of fundamental information about job situations and future trend is   21._____
    A. *The Occupation Index*
    B. *Occupational Outlook Handbook*
    C. *Dictionary of Occupational Titles*
    D. *Career Briefs*

22. It was decided recently to screen all potential draftees far before induction. The purpose of this step was to   22._____
    A. increase the number of volunteers
    B. get the unemployed off the streets
    C. get a better picture of the manpower skills available
    D. provide remedial help to people who fail the induction tests

23. The employment picture in our country is in a state of rapid change. In which one of the following states is employment increasing MOST rapidly?   23._____
    A. Illinois   B. Oregon
    C. New York   D. Texas

24. Of the following, which is the correct statement of a current occupational trend?   24._____
    A. The geographic movement of workers is increasing
    B. The population is increasing, but the available labor force is decreasing
    C. The proportion of workers aged 45 and over is decreasing
    D. The proportion of workers providing services is decreasing

5 (#1)

25. The manpower outlook in large cities in the years 1980 through 1990 indicated a decline in the
    A. number of persons in the resident labor force under age 25
    B. number of semi-skilled jobs
    C. number of females in the resident labor force
    D. proportion of the population accounted for by non-whites

25._____

KEY (CORRECT ANSWERS)

1. C	11. D	21. B
2. C	12. A	22. D
3. A	13. A	23. D
4. B	14. C	24. A
5. D	15. B	25. B
6. A	16. B	
7. D	17. A	
8. A	18. A	
9. D	19. A	
10. D	20. D	

TEST 2

DIRECTIONS: Each question or incomplete statement is followed by several suggested answers or completions. Select the one that BEST answers the question or completes the statement. *PRINT THE LETTER OF THE CORRECT ANSWER IN THE SPACE AT THE RIGHT.*

1. The term "vocational development" is preferred to that of "vocational choice" by one of the following persons. He claims that in deciding on an occupation, one is choosing a means of implementing a self-concept; he claims, also, that the individual goes through various "life stages" in so doing. He is
   A. Ginzberg
   B. Axelrod
   C. Karnes
   D. Super

   1._____

2. If present trends continue, what percentage of all workers in the U.S. will be women?
   A. 50%   B. 25%   C. 33%   D. 66%

   2._____

3. Which one of the following occupational groups is MOST responsive to rises and falls in the business cycles?
   A. Professionals
   B. Craftsmen and foremen
   C. Semi-skilled workers
   D. Clerical workers

   3._____

4. The more generally used forms of the *Kuder Preference Record—Occupational* contain nine or ten scales, each of which reflects an area or cluster of activity, such as mechanical, social service or clerical. The *Strong Vocational Interest Blank*, on the other hand, is typified by an approach which uses criterion groups of
   A. pre- and post-college individuals whose academic majors, interests and competencies are a clear matter of record
   B. successfully employed men in a variety of occupations whose responses are compared to a presumably representative group of men in general
   C. children at various social-class levels, whose interests and actual careers have been followed up subsequently for more than 25 years
   D. superior and marginal achievers in a large number of professions and sub-professions

   4._____

5. Occupational information which specifies hiring standards is known as the
   A. job specification   B. job description
   C. job analysis   D. occupational analysis

   5._____

6. State Employment Service interviewers classify experienced applicants according to
    A. the job opportunities available
    B. abilities and skills
    C. physical capacities
    D. educational background

7. Related jobs can more easily be located in the *Dictionary of Occupational Titles* in Part
    A. I   B. II   C. III   D. IV

8. Of the following broad areas of work in which people are engaged, the one in which MOST workers are employed is
    A. clerical work
    B. farming
    C. semi-skilled work
    D. selling

9. The proportion of the total working force engaged in certain broad occupational fields has shifted markedly in the period from 1910 to the present. Of the following, the field in which there has been the greatest increase is
    A. farm workers
    B. service workers
    C. laborers
    D. clerks and salespeople

10. Social Security or Old Age and Survivors Insurance is paid for by
    A. taxes deducted from the employee's salary only
    B. funds set aside by the federal government from income taxes
    C. the state in which the worker lives at the time of his retirement or death
    D. taxes deducted from the employee's salary plus an equal amount paid by the employer

11. If a counselor wishes to provide vocational guidance using as one basis an occupational-interest test, he must FIRST be certain the test has _____ validity.
    A. content
    B. predictive
    C. concurrent
    D. construct

12. Strong recently reported that a group of engineers responded to the Vocational Interest Inventory in the same manner as they had 20 years before. We may conclude from this that the test demonstrates adequate
    A. reliability
    B. validity
    C. usefulness
    D. efficiency

13. One of the major new emphases in vocational counseling which has been stressed by Gilbert Wrenn and others is that
    A. the counselor helps the student define goals, not merely to inventory capacities
    B. more women are going to be working in the future
    C. talent must be looked at in terms of its marketable value
    D. the counselor must stress the fact that satisfying occupations are decreasing

14. Unemployment has particularly affected the disadvantaged groups. For example, compared with a national average rate of about 6%, unemployment among teenage Puerto Ricans in New York City runs about
    A. 2%   B. 5%   C. 10%   D. 40%

15. Job mobility is an important factor in labor force dynamics. Which of the following groups has the highest proportion of persons who change their jobs in the course of a year?
    A. Unskilled laborers
    B. Clerical workers
    C. Professional and technical personnel
    D. Sales workers

16. In Menninger's view, which one of the following factors accounts for the greatest number of job dismissals?
    A. Technical incompetence
    B. Inability to relate to other workers
    C. Inability to relate to authority figures
    D. Poor work habits

17. Among American industries, there is much variation with regard to the unemployment experience of the workforce. Which one of the following major industry divisions generally has the highest unemployment rate?
    A. Agriculture
    B. Construction
    C. Trade
    D. Manufacturing

18. The only major industry division which is expected to decline in the next decade is
    A. mining
    B. agriculture
    C. manufacturing
    D. transportation and public utilities

    18._____

19. The incidence of unemployment varies significantly by industry. The highest unemployment rates are found in which American industry division?
    A. Manufacturing
    B. Construction
    C. Trade
    D. Government

    19._____

20. During the next ten years, job opportunities in government, in relation to total labor force growth, is expected to show the following change:
    A. more than average
    B. average
    C. less than average
    D. no change

    20._____

21. Job opportunities are growing fastest in jobs requiring the most education; nevertheless, in 2000, what proportion of the labor force had NOT completed high school?
    A. More than 70 percent
    B. More than 50 percent
    C. More than 30 percent
    D. More than 10 percent

    21._____

22. *Occupational Outlook Handbook* is a publication of the
    A. Vocational Advisory Service
    B. United States Bureau of Labor Statistics
    C. Welfare Council
    D. Vocational Counselors' Association

    22._____

23. What is the general relationship of unemployment rates for non-white and white workers?
    A. Lower for non-whites
    B. About the same
    C. Twice as high for non-whites
    D. Five times as high for non-whites

    23._____

24. Teenagers' unemployment experience, in relationship to the rest of the labor force, is evidenced in an unemployment rate which bears what relationship to the average for all groups?
    A. Three times as high
    B. Twice as high
    C. Fifty percent higher
    D. About the same

24._____

25. The highest unemployment rate experienced by any labor force category is found among which ONE of the following groups?
    A. Unskilled laborers
    B. Women
    C. High school dropouts
    D. Non-white teenage girls

25._____

KEY (CORRECT ANSWERS)

1. D	11. B	21. C
2. A	12. A	22. B
3. C	13. A	23. C
4. B	14. D	24. A
5. A	15. A	25. C
6. B	16. B	
7. B	17. B	
8. C	18. A	
9. D	19. B	
10. D	20. A	

EXAMINATION SECTION
TEST 1

DIRECTIONS: Each question or incomplete statement is followed by several suggested answers or completions. Select the one that BEST answers the question or completes the statement. *PRINT THE LETTER OF THE CORRECT ANSWER IN THE SPACE AT THE RIGHT.*

Questions 1-3.

DIRECTIONS: Answer Questions 1 to 3 based on the following situation.

You are a school counselor in an academic and commercial high school. A senior boy by the name of Peter informs you that for years he has wished to prepare for the practice of medicine. His parents urged him to make this choice when an uncle, who was a doctor, promised to pay part of his college expenses, provided he enrolled in the medical course.

You have listened with interest to Peter's problem as he related it. You have talked to all of his teachers, studied his school records, checked his grades, and given him a battery of tests. All of his grades were below average. Tests revealed that he had slightly less than an average mental ability. Personality and adjustment tests revealed nothing wrong except a slight tendency to be dissatisfied with his family relationship. His clerical aptitude test score was low. Three mechanical aptitude tests, however, revealed high promise. Further questioning revealed that for years Peter had tinkered in his own shop with tools.

It appears that unwise family pressures had caused Peter to choose a life work beyond his ability to achieve.

1. Your FIRST step in handling this problem should be to

    A. tell the parents that they must agree to a search for another life goal
    B. inform the boy's parents that their son does not have the ability to succeed in a profession
    C. confer with the boy's parents and get them to, have the boy keep trying to gain entrance to a medical school
    D. see the boy's parents and suggest that they forget about his choice of a vocation for the present

2. You later arranged a meeting with Peter and during your interview with him, he stated that he wanted to learn more about various types of work before he chose. Under these conditions, you should

    A. advise him to take a variety of subjects as tryouts so that he will be able to make a wiser choice
    B. suggest that he learn something about the requirements of other jobs
    C. take him to the library and show him books to read on various types of work and try to given him insight into his abilities and interests
    D. tell him you feel that he is old enough to decide now

1.____

2.____

35

3. After thinking about it, Peter finally decided to prepare for work as a garage mechanic. You should then

   A. advise him to change to a trade school and take auto mechanics or machine shop and do that kind of work during the summer
   B. advise him to drop chemistry and biology but not give up completely the idea of becoming a doctor
   C. advise him to remain in school and take several more science subjects
   D. try to interest him in getting a job in a garage and attending night school

4. You are a judge in a juvenile court in a large city. A young girl fifteen years of age is brought before you. She is charged with the theft of a dress, perfume, and handbag from a large department store. The total value of the articles is $437. This is the first time the girl has been caught. She is from a middle class family. Her mother works in a factory in the daytime, and her father is employed in a local bank as an assistant cashier. Their combined income is about $40,000 a year. She is an only child. Her school record is good, and one test showed that she had better than average mental ability.
   After having had a talk with the girl, it is your duty to make a decision. You FIRST would

   A. give her a severe scolding and release her, but make her pay the bill
   B. counsel with the girl and her parents and then give her another chance
   C. talk with the mother to find out whether the girl had ever been neglected
   D. inform the girl that you are thinking of sending her to a girls' training school

5. Wally is a bright five-year-old boy in a kindergarten group. Every day he wastes the time of the group by being slow in putting away materials at the end of the activity period. You, his teacher, know that at home his toys are picked up and put away by his mother or father when he tires of them. He is an only child.
   You should

   A. tell his parents to force him to pick up things at home so that he will put away his materials when he is at school
   B. tell him to hurry because the group is waiting for him
   C. help him to put away his materials so the group will not be forced to wait
   D. send the group to the gymnasium to play a game which Wally likes, and have Wally lose out on the fun while he puts away his materials

6. Jimmy, a first-grade pupil, is active on the playground. In the schoolroom, however, he refuses to take part and frequently cries when told to do so.
   In trying to remedy this situation, you, as his teacher, should

   A. advise him to take part at once because you think that he is afraid
   B. ask his parents to keep him at home for a year in the belief that he is not yet mature enough to begin school
   C. keep harmony in the class by permitting him to take part when he chooses to do so
   D. encourage him to take part gradually

7. Ralph, who is in the sixth grade, likes to make things with tools and seems to enjoy helping you keep the library books in order and the room decorated nicely. He finds arithmetic very difficult and often avoids it. He plays truant quite often.
   In handling this truancy problem, you should

A. discuss why his offense is serious and try to get him to see the error of his ways
B. attempt to discover the causes of his difficulty and tell him you will excuse him from arithmetic if he does not skip school
C. compliment him on his mechanical ability and at the proper time assign him mechanical work in which arithmetic would be useful
D. tell him that staying out of school is an offense not to be tolerated

8. Harry sprinkled a foul-smelling drug around the classroom. The odor was so bad that it made some of the pupils ill and thus almost broke up school for the day. When the teacher discovered who did it, she forced Harry to apologize to the school and to stand before the class each morning for a week taking a smell of the drug from a vial which she kept in her possession.
In your judgment, this form of punishment

   A. will cure him
   B. is not quite severe enough for the offense
   C. was carried on too long even though it produced the desired results
   D. is apt to fail

9. For more than a month, various articles had been disappearing from the lockers in the school hallway. Finally, the instructor caught Jerry going through the coats in the lockers. He admitted the thefts. The instructor knew that Jerry's parents were very poor. He had no spending money, and his meals did not meet his needs.
His instructor should

   A. give him a weekly amount which he can pay back sometime and also give him an apple, a sandwich, or candy when possible
   B. help him find work so that he can take care of his own needs
   C. show him that a thief always gets caught and then promise him a still worse penalty if he does it again
   D. make an example of him by telling the students that he stole the articles

10. Jack, in the eighth grade, is always doing something to attract the attention of his classmates. He makes *bright* remarks during class, insists on talking more than his share of the time, acts up as he walks around the room to obtain a laugh, and even dresses, walks, and combs his hair in an unusual manner to attract attention.
His teachers think that

    A. he should be separated from the group or otherwise punished until he learns not to disturb
    B. the best way to handle him is to join with his classmates in smiling at his remarks and tricks because this cannot do a great deal of harm
    C. the teacher should give him the attention he desires whenever he earns it by doing something worthwhile
    D. the teacher should refuse to notice his behavior so it will return to normal again

11. The teacher has noticed lately that Mildred, age eight, answers out of turn, speaks when others are speaking, and wants to be the center of attention in every activity. She pouts or cries if another child is selected to do something for the teacher which she wishes to do. She has no sister but has a new baby brother.
The MOST probable explanation of her behavior is that

A. her behavior changed because she now has new duties at home
B. she is no longer the center of attention at home and is seeking more attention at school
C. she is being disobedient because she has been spoiled from babyhood
D. Mildred is probably suffering from some illness

12. You are an employment officer. It is your duty to talk with and refer individuals who are trying to secure work. There have been many inquiries regarding a particularly fine automotive mechanic's job in a well-known shop in the city. It offers a good chance to anyone who obtains it. It is up to you to fill this opening from a large group of men applying for this work.
You should select the man who

   A. showed that he knew his trade and showed you the best set of written references and recommendations from his former employers
   B. appeared to be most highly recommended by such previous employers as you were able to contact and answered the trade questions most satisfactorily
   C. told you he had the best training and had the longest experience in the automotive field
   D. appeared the most intelligent and answered the oral trade questions correctly

13. As head nurse in a leading hospital, you are faced with a serious problem. Two of your very efficient nurses are unable to cooperate and to avoid trouble. You have attempted to improve the situation by talking to both of them but their attitudes and relations have not improved.
It would be BEST to

   A. dismiss the less efficient nurse and secure a more satisfactory employee to take her position
   B. overlook their attitude toward each other as much as possible
   C. assign each to unpleasant duties and thereby attempt to teach both that they should try to cooperate better with each other
   D. place them on duty in different wards of the hospital so that they will not need to work together

14. You are a nurse in a city hospital assigned to a patient who demands too much of your time, thus causing you to neglect other duties.
The situation would BEST be handled agreeably by

   A. referring her case to the hospital authorities
   B. doing things requested by her to avoid offending her
   C. explaining pleasantly but firmly why you are unable to grant all of her requests
   D. paying no attention to her occasionally so she will not ask so often

15. You are a social case worker from a public welfare agency. You are charged with advising and assisting poor families which supposedly are in need of financial or medical aid. You are asked to investigate a family of six small children whose father is a ne'er-do-well and who is in a drunken condition most of the time. The mother has been frail and sickly for years.
Under these conditions, you should

   A. give them a monthly allowance despite the father's drinking
   B. refuse them all help so that the father might feel forced to work

C. take the children from the family and advise the mother to secure a divorce
D. give them a monthly allowance and have the father sent to a sanitarium or other institution for medical help

16. Virginia is an attractive girl in the ninth grade with ability somewhat above the average. She is nervous and worries a great deal about her schoolwork and about life in general. Her mother is very anxious for her to excel in school. She criticizes Virginia if her marks are not high and urges her to work harder.
If you were Virginia's teacher, the method you would use in helping Virginia is to

   A. show the other pupils what fine work Virginia is doing, using her case as a model to inspire the others
   B. talk to the mother, explaining that it may be dangerous to urge Virginia to earn high marks
   C. encourage Virginia and her mother to continue as at present since it is likely to lead to high scholarship
   D. tell Virginia that she should not study hard

16.____

17. The attitudes of three teachers in discussing the behavior of their pupils is shown in the four paragraphs that follow.
Which do you regard as BEST from the standpoint of development of the child?

   A. When a child does what is wrong, he should be withdrawn from the group so that he may think over his poor behavior.
   B. Teachers should watch children, stopping them promptly the instant they get into mischief. Privileges should be temporarily withdrawn because of offenses.
   C. When a child misbehaves, he should be punished.
   D. When a child misbehaves, the adult should explain what the right mode of behavior is and why it is right.

17.____

18. Teacher X will never admit that she is wrong. Every question in the classroom is taken as a challenge to her authority. Every comment on her work is regarded as unfair criticism. She makes sarcastic comments to her fellow workers but never apologizes. She can usually prove to her own satisfaction that she is right. She interrupts friends or students so often that no one is able to finish a discussion in her presence.
If you were the principal, you would

   A. put up with the behavior since in a few more years she will be obliged to retire
   B. tell her that she may lose her position if she does not change
   C. have a serious talk with her and force her to see her behavior is educationally unsound
   D. arrange for a psychiatrist to help her to understand her behavior and alter it

18.____

19. Dale shows shyness on the playground. He seems afraid to enter into the games and is so awkward when he plays that the boys do not like to choose him on their side. You are the director.
How can you assist him in overcoming this fear? You should

   A. give him some easy task connected with the games, such as keeping score
   B. allow him to watch or to do something with another pupil
   C. advise him to learn to play
   D. insist that he get into the games and play

19.____

20. A ten-year-old boy in the fourth grade suddenly begins to stutter. He is ashamed, and the children in his class are amused.
    The teacher should
    A. advise the parents to keep him out of school for a while because of his nervousness
    B. compel him to recite in front of the class so that he will cure his stuttering
    C. tell him he can stop if he wants to and then attempt to overlook the condition if it occurs again
    D. refer him to a clinic for help

20.____

KEY (CORRECT ANSWERS)

1.	D	11.	B
2.	C	12.	B
3.	A	13.	D
4.	B	14.	C
5.	D	15.	D
6.	D	16.	B
7.	C	17.	D
8.	D	18.	D
9.	B	19.	A
10.	C	20.	D

TEST 2

DIRECTIONS: Each question or incomplete statement is followed by several suggested answers or completions. Select the one that BEST answers the question or completes the statement. *PRINT THE LETTER OF THE CORRECT ANSWER IN THE SPACE AT THE RIGHT.*

Questions 1-8.

DIRECTIONS: If you were judging social workers, which of the following personality traits would you consider the MOST important for a successful person in this type of work? Select ONE in each group, and mark its letter in the space at the right.

1. A. Aggressive and persuasive
   B. Determined and hard working
   C. Prudent and careful
   D. Helpful and kindly

2. A. Ambitious and spirited
   B. Tactful and diplomatic
   C. Persuasive and overbearing
   D. Cautious and prudent

3. A. *Slippery* and critical
   B. Pleasant appearing and apologetic
   C. Selfish and self-reliant
   D. Well-balanced and interested in people

4. A. Persevering and determined
   B. Considerate and understanding
   C. Outstanding and superior
   D. Friendly and spirited

5. A. Sympathetic and condescending
   B. Determined and superior
   C. Practical and experienced
   D. Self-confident and changeable

6. A. Sociable and sincere
   B. Self-reliant and theoretical
   C. Overbearing and forward
   D. Agreeable and congenial

7. A. Self-confident and assured
   B. Energetic and tactless
   C. Intelligent and ambitious
   D. Industrious and tolerant

8. A. Enthusiastic and eager
   B. Cheerful and apologetic
   C. Cordial and tolerant
   D. Analytical and intelligent

9. Geraldine, a junior in high school, is boasting constantly about something that she has done, or about the members of her family. Her companions think that she is conceited. A close study of her case shows the following possibilities.
   The MOST likely cause of her boastful conduct is that

   A. her father is a prominent man in town, highly respected by his fellow citizens
   B. she has ability above the average and generally earns good marks
   C. she lacks self-confidence and occasionally hints to her teacher that she is not quite as capable as her classmates
   D. she has been spoiled by having had too much attention

10. Skippy, a high school senior, is a poor athlete. No matter how hard he tries, he seems unable to do well in sports. This worries him. He has expressed the opinion that he does not amount to much. He has had a physical examination and his poor athletic ability is not due to physical causes. Skippy can *probably* be helped if

    A. his teachers urge him to put forth every effort to become good in athletics
    B. teachers let him alone to fight the battle that everyone must fight sooner or later when he learns that someone else is better than he
    C. his teachers study his case and help him to discover other things that he can do well
    D. the coach places him in a special class known as the awkward squad and teaches him to improve his athletic ability

11. In order to help a child to avoid developing the feeling that others are ALWAYS better than he is, you should

    A. assist him in becoming as successful as possible in the things he attempts
    B. try to get him to see that he is as competent as anyone else
    C. tell him never to admit that he is beaten
    D. help him to be as successful as possible in the things he attempts and help him to do some one thing especially well

12. With pupils of extremely low mental ability, it is MOST justifiable to

    A. give them the same work as the others get but realize that it will take them longer to do it
    B. give them the same type of work as the others get but less of it
    C. assign more extra curricular work and less from the regular curriculum; for example, use more handwork
    D. place all of them in manual arts courses

13. You are a personnel manager in a large industrial plant engaged in the manufacture of vital instruments. It is your job to maintain good employee-employer relationships, increase the amount of work done, and keep the men happy and satisfied in their work. In other words, you are active in keeping up high standards of work by keeping everyone happy.
    One of your experienced employees, Mr. Ryan, is engaged in the final inspection of shuttle o-rings. He apparently has fallen down in his work rating without any known reason. He holds an important job and must maintain a high degree of skill. The plant physician, after a thorough physical examination, says there is nothing wrong with him physically.
    Under these conditions, you should

A. suggest that he might lose his job if he does not increase the quality and amount of work he does
B. talk with him and attempt to determine what is causing his trouble or what is worrying him
C. drop a word of praise occasionally so he might be helped to do better
D. suggest that it might help if he changed to a different type of work

14. Suppose that you found that Mr. Ryan was upset at work because of difficulties with his wife and his envy of a man who was promoted over him.
You should

A. try to explain to him why this man was promoted over him
B. to satisfy him, tell him that your plant promotes those first who were employed first, and casually suggest that his wife drop in to see you
C. give him some marital advice and suggest that he may be better off if he separated from his wife for a while
D. tell him you are interested only in his output and that he will have to work out his personal affairs by himself

14._____

15. You are a Red Cross director with an army unit in the field. A soldier, Jones, approaches you and tells you there is serious illness in his family, and he would like to go home. You agree, but upon looking into the matter the next day, you find that no one is actually sick in the soldier's family.
Under these conditions, you should

A. take no further action at present but later get the man a furlough because you can see that he is under serious strain and may become very ill
B. treat it as a humorous incident but be on the lookout so that it does not occur again
C. notify the commanding officer and get his opinion
D. deny the request and try to find out the real cause for the man's behavior

15._____

16. If Jones then saw you again, you should

A. tell him to pour out his troubles to you
B. scold him for his actions and explain the seriousness of such dishonesty
C. explain that taking vacations whenever he feels like it is impossible; offer assistance and try to find something to interest him
D. explain to him in a nice manner that you have shortened his furlough a few days

16._____

17. Jones then told you that he was sick and tired of the army and wanted to get away from it for a while.
You should

A. warn him of what would happen if he deserted and obtain a furlough for him
B. notify his commanding officer that the man should be watched
C. suggest an appointment be made for him with the psychiatrist
D. refuse to interest yourself in his problem because it is not your concern

17._____

18. If Jones also told you that his first sergeant was picking on him, you should

A. look into the matter to determine the truth by talking to a few people who know him
B. call the soldier's commanding officer and tell him about the situation

18._____

C. tell him to forget the incident since it really was not very serious
D. try to arrange to get the soldier transferred to another company

19. You are a dean in a secondary school. An intelligent child, Bob, sixteen years of age who is about to fail, has been referred to you. Prior to this time, the boy has been a good student and a very likable boy. Suddenly, he began to neglect his work.
Under these conditions, you should

   A. go to the principal and suggest that the boy be deprived of a few privileges around school until his behavior improves
   B. have a casual talk with the boy
   C. learn about the boy's home life and outside activities
   D. have a talk with the boy and tell him he must apply himself

20. If you should have a talk with Bob, your FIRST step will be to try to

   A. make him feel that by improving his behavior it will please you
   B. gain his confidence so he will feel free to tell his problem
   C. impress him with the importance of your position
   D. show him that he is developing some bad habits

21. You discover that one reason for Bob's poor attitude is the fact that he feels he is being left out of things.
Knowing this, you should

   A. ask his friends to aid him in his studies
   B. force him to engage in sports
   C. tell him not to worry as things are bound to turn out all right
   D. seek the help of his friends

22. If, in two months, you heard nothing more concerning Bob, you should

   A. have one of his teachers send him to you
   B. look into his current activities and then drop in and talk to him about how well he is progressing in his classes and social relations
   C. inquire about him and then drop in casually and observe him
   D. look at his school record to determine whether he had improved

23. Near the close of the school year, you notice a great improvement in Bob's behavior, and his grades have improved.
You then should

   A. call the boy in and tell him you were disappointed in the amount of improvement shown because you knew he could do better
   B. say nothing to him but inform his parents that he has improved
   C. go to him and comment on his splendid improvement
   D. give him a two-day holiday as a reward for the splendid improvement shown

24. Which of these teacher's opinions is CORRECT?

   A. Mr. W. - "I think some children are naturally quite mischievous and must be dealt with sternly."
   B. Mr. X. - "I have a pupil who causes a great deal of trouble. After I scold him, he quiets down and behaves himself."

C. Mr. Y. - *"Since every bit of misconduct has a cause, we should not be angry with a child who misbehaves any more than we should get angry at one who is ill. "*
D. Mr. Z. - *"Most misconduct can be traced right back to the home. It is the parents' fault."*

25. You are a social case worker from a public welfare agency. One of your cases is Mr. Backus, an aged man whose failing health makes nursing care necessary.
Mr. Backus is dependent upon relief. An agency reports that he suffers from *senility and paralysis*. His only son is confined in the Veterans Hospital. There are no other relatives. Mr. Backus is receiving $320 per month, but he feels he should be receiving at least $600 per month on which to live since the high cost of living makes it very hard to get along on less. He has no savings. His landlady says that she does not wish to have him remain there because she cannot care for an invalid.
After a complete investigation of this case, you then should

   A. arrange to increase Mr. Backus' pension to $600 a month and then try to get the landlady to keep him
   B. place him in a home for old people at public expense
   C. increase his pension to $600 a month and make arrangements with the owner of a nursing home to care for Mr. Backus
   D. try to have the son support him

KEY (CORRECT ANSWERS)

1.	D		11.	D
2.	B		12.	C
3.	D		13.	B
4.	B		14.	A
5.	C		15.	D
6.	A		16.	C
7.	D		17.	C
8.	C		18.	A
9.	C		19.	C
10.	C		20.	B

21. D
22. B
23. C
24. C
25. C

EXAMINATION SECTION
TEST 1

DIRECTIONS: Each question or incomplete statement is followed by several suggested answers or completions. Select the one that BEST answers the question or completes the statement. *PRINT THE LETTER OF THE CORRECT ANSWER IN THE SPACE AT THE RIGHT.*

1. In working to establish whether a client is a definite job-counseling case, a counselor's most important clue is

   A. the counselor's overall evaluation of what the client has said so far, plus an evaluation of nonverbal since the interview started
   B. the feelings, needs, or pressures indicated by the client's words
   C. any comments or recommendations made by a referring professional
   D. the client's statement of her problem

2. Which of the following types of clients would MOST likely be experiencing severe financial problems?

   A. Culturally different clients
   B. Former military personnel
   C. Displaced homemakers
   D. Voluntary *midlife changers*

3. Which of the following multiple attitude tests is generally considered by job counseling professionals to be the most well-researched?

   A. Differential Aptitude Test (DAT)
   B. Flanagan Aptitude Classification Test (FACT)
   C. General Aptitude Test Battery (GATB)
   D. Otis-Lennon Mental Ability Test (OLMAT)

4. Approximately what percentage of the job-seeking population knows what they want to do for a living or what jobs match their needs?

   A. 5-10   B. 20-30   C. 25-40   D. 50-70

5. Which of the following is/are poor choices for an on-the-job tryout?
   I. An engineering student who is encountering difficulty in choosing among research, applied, sales, and training options
   II. A recent GED recipient who wants to learn about the responsibilities of a paralegal assistant
   III. A high school graduate who wants to learn about the work of a night custodian
   IV. A college graduate with a biology degree who wants to learn about the different types of work in the field of nursing

   The CORRECT answer is:

   A. I, II
   B. II, IV
   C. I, III, IV
   D. All of the above

1.____

2.____

3.____

4.____

5.____

6. Which of the following statements about newspaper want ads is FALSE?
They

   A. typically represent hiring by last resort
   B. typically account for about 30–40% of the job leads that result in work
   C. tend to be skewed toward low-paying, high-turnover jobs and highly specialized occupations
   D. are usually the first place job seekers should look for jobs

7. Ideally, any *small talk* that is used to make a job–seeking client comfortable during an initial meeting should be

   A. of mutual interest
   B. centered on the client
   C. neutral
   D. focused on the counselor

8. Which of the following are significant DISADVANTAGES associated with seeking job search or career advice from employers and other experts?
   I. Such appearances or interviews rarely lead to concrete job leads and may be considered a waste of time by clients or students.
   II. Unhappy or burned–out advisers may discourage qualified and able applicants.
   III. Each expert is a potential source of personal prejudice.

   The CORRECT answer is:

   A. I only
   B. I, II
   C. II, III
   D. All of the above

9. Which of the following questions is considered to be unlawful during a job interview?

   A. Where do you live?
   B. How old are you?
   C. Which languages other than English are you able to read, write or speak?
   D. Have you ever used another name?

10. Which of the following is NOT a guideline for using want ads in a job search?

    A. *Apply in person* means an applicant may call if he or she does not own car.
    B. Want ads addresses and phone numbers are usually all right to apply for.
    C. Sunday papers are a good source of want ads for the next week.
    D. It may be a good idea to write one's own *job wanted* ad to let employers know they have skills and want work.

11. Typically, it takes about _____ mass–mailed resumes for a job seeker to get one interview offer.

    A. 10
    B. 70
    C. 120
    D. 250

12. A counselor often works with clients who are described as *disadvantaged*—a broad term encompassing cultural, educational, environmental, economic, physical, social, and psychological deprivation. Each of the following is typical of the communication pattern of such clients, EXCEPT it is

    A. temporal rather than spatial
    B. physical and visual rather than auditory
    C. externally oriented, rather than introspective
    D. inductive, rather than deductive

13. Although the Americans With Disabilities Act and most state laws permit employers to use pre-employment medical examinations, they must meet certain requirements. Which of the following is NOT typically one of these?
They

    A. must be applied uniformly to all applicants
    B. must be conducted after an offer of employment is extended
    C. may not include a test for the HIV virus or AIDS
    D. must be job-related

14. Which of the following tests is most appropriate for measuring the readiness of individuals to make choices about vocational issues?

    A. Differential Aptitude Tests (DAT)
    B. Kuder General Interest Survey
    C. Guilford-Zimmerman Survey
    D. Career Development Inventory (CDI)

15. A career professional wants to allow a client to perform a work tryout, but feels that encountering the negative feelings of others employed in the work setting could be very damaging to the client. The counselor's BEST course would be to involve the client in a _____ program.

    A. volunteer work experience
    B. cooperative education
    C. simulated work experience
    D. work-study

16. The MOST commonly used type of educational media in vocational counseling is/are

    A. computer-assisted guidance
    B. programmed instructional materials
    C. printed matter
    D. audio-visual media

17. Which of the following is NOT a significant difference between group career counseling and group career guidance? Group

    A. guidance is only indirectly concerned with attitudes and behaviors
    B. counseling is intended for clients with temporary problems which require more than mere information
    C. guidance procedures can more often be used with large groups
    D. counseling is intended to be instructional; group guidance deals with self-discovery

18. The typical job search involves about _____ rejections for each single offer to be interviewed.

    A. 5   B. 15   C. 30   D. 50

19. According to the Employment and Training ADMINISTRATION'S DICTIONARY OF OCCUPATIONAL TITLES (DOT), which of the following is an operative?

    A. Garbage collector
    B. Machinist
    C. Welder
    D. Carpenter

20. Which of the following should be avoided when preparing a resume?

    A. Focusing on the needs and aspirations of the job seeker
    B. Writing short sentences and statements
    C. Using examples to illustrate skills or abilities
    D. Using type style, headings, and bullets (•) to accentuate certain elements

21. Which of the following is a personality/attitude assessment that is suggested as appropriate for individuals of college age and older?

    A. Otis–Lennon Mental Ability Test (OLMAT)
    B. Edwards Personal Preference Schedule (EPPS)
    C. Ohio Vocational Interest Survey (OVIS, OVIS II)
    D. Work Values Inventory (WVI)

22. Essentially, there are three major purposes for an initial job seeker/counselor interview. Which of the following is NOT one of these?

    A. Agreeing on the structure and plan for further counseling and related activities
    B. Establishing a relationship so that counseling can continue
    C. Suggesting possible areas of career exploration
    D. Establishing the client's needs and feelings

23. Which of the following is a functional job skill?

    A. Tolerating stress   B. Persistence
    C. Imagination   D. Writing

24. When a client or student names and describes a *dream job,* each of the following is an important response in the early stages of a job search EXCEPT

    A. linking his/her aspirations with immediate, practical steps toward the long–term goal
    B. reinforcing or validating the dream choice
    C. finding out why he/she chose it
    D. cautioning him/her if the job seems outrageous or impractical

25. Educational media in vocational counseling tend to be LEAST effective when

    A. they are introduced carefully and conspicuously into the program
    B. they are applied to small, isolated educational problems
    C. the media developer and the counselor select materials together
    D. they are integrated into the entire program

KEY (CORRECT ANSWERS)

1. A
2. C
3. C
4. B
5. B

6. D
7. A
8. C
9. B
10. A

11. D
12. A
13. C
14. D
15. C

16. C
17. D
18. B
19. C
20. A

21. B
22. C
23. D
24. D
25. B

TEST 2

DIRECTIONS: Each question or incomplete statement is followed by several suggested answers or completions. Select the one that BEST answers the question or completes the statement. *PRINT THE LETTER OF THE CORRECT ANSWER IN THE SPACE AT THE RIGHT.*

1. Which of the following statements about interviewing for a job is TRUE?
   A. A screening interviewer is looking for a reason to accept a candidate, rather than a reason to reject him.
   B. In a nondirective interview, a candidate is permitted to talk about anything he likes.
   C. A candidate should volunteer nothing in a screening interview.
   D. Interviewers will never intentionally introduce stress into an interview situation.

2. Each of the following are disadvantages associated with a holistic life–career planning process EXCEPT
   A. it does not address the important issue of a job seeker's marketable skills
   B. it can overemphasize the nature of individual decision–making
   C. it tends to equate one's worth and life with his work
   D. the possibility of making a poor choice is much more frightening to first–time job seekers

3. When an employer begins to hire and is considering potential employees, she is typically LEAST concerned with
   A. the number of years or months of work experience that is directly related to the position
   B. whether a candidate will be easy to train
   C. whether a candidate will stay on the job after being trained
   D. the quality of a candidate's work habits

4. It is generally agreed that job counselors use standardized tests for a few specific purposes. Which of the following is NOT one of these?
   A. Diagnosis
   B. Prediction
   C. Placement
   D. Monitoring

5. In general, 70–90% of employees who are fired from their jobs are let go because
   A. their job skills are poorly matched to the position
   B. they have inappropriate social skills or poor work habits
   C. they have committed one or more serious and costly errors
   D. they cannot handle the workload

6. According to the Employment and Training ADMINISTRATION'S DICTIONARY OF OCCUPATIONAL TITLES (DOT), which of the following is a benchwork occupation?
   A. Bank teller
   B. Sheet–metal worker
   C. Piano tuner
   D. Punch press operator

7. Once a job seeker has been taught phone skills, he or she should call each employer_____ before considering the job lead *dead*.
   A. once
   B. twice
   C. three times
   D. five times

8. In general, which of the following can be defined as the ultimate outcomes or goals of job search training?
    I. Learning how to find employers by networking and persistence
    II. Selecting a life-long career in the field of one's primary interest
    III. Learning how to describe one's interests and marketable skills in a positive and detailed manner

    The CORRECT answer is:

    A. I only
    B. II only
    C. I, III
    D. All of the above

9. Each of the following is a way in which work experience programs can increase the motivation for learning in disadvantaged clients EXCEPT

    A. developing specific occupational skills
    B. increasing feelings of self-worth
    C. leading to specific job leads
    D. helping clients find the financial assistance needed to remain in school

10. Which of the following is a disadvantage associated with the use of the Flanagan Aptitude Classification Test (FACT) for determining a client's vocational skills?

    A. Test accessories tend to be badly organized and sketchy.
    B. Tests are usually not considered to be interesting or challenging.
    C. The basic assumption of measuring identified job elements and combining test of those basic elements to estimate possible success does not always appear logical.
    D. It is of limited value for clients who are considering occupations that require college preparation.

11. The ideal time for a job seeker to give her resume to a potential employer is

    A. on the first contact, with an explanatory letter
    B. after making an appointment for a personal interview
    C. right at the beginning of a personal interview
    D. after a personal interview

12. Which of the following behaviors is most likely to make an applicant appear overly familiar during an interview?

    A. Raised eyebrows
    B. Shuffling feet
    C. Shrugging
    D. Leaning back

13. Which of the following is an adaptive job skill?

    A. Planning
    B. Analyzing
    C. Being courteous
    D. Memorizing

14. A rule of thumb for resume preparation is that about _____% of the page should remain blank or empty.

    A. 5
    B. 10
    C. 30
    D. 50

15. Each of the following is an important difference between technical and nontechnical skills in the job market EXCEPT

   A. technical skills set the basic requirements for a job
   B. all jobs require a variety of nontechnical skills
   C. nontechnical skills determine success beyond a basic level
   D. all jobs have readily identifiable technical skills

16. The main problem with using printed and audio-visual materials as educational media in job counseling is that they

   A. may move the client too quickly through the job-choice process
   B. retain their usability longer than their accuracy
   C. tend to restrict the role of the counselor
   D. may present too much information to a client at once

17. Which of the following career/job search materials or resources is most likely to be used at the latest phase in the selection process?

   A. Work tryout experience
   B. Printed guidance materials
   C. Interviews with trainers
   D. Computerized materials

18. While many clients have difficulty finding a job right away, some clients fail to find a job at all. Each of the following is usually involved in such a situation EXCEPT

   A. the client is not sure about how to begin an effective job search
   B. there are few to no jobs in the client's particular field of interest or expertise
   C. the client gives up looking for work too soon
   D. the client feels that there are many weak points in his/her past

19. When working with a job seeker who is an ex-offender or drug addict, the BEST course of action is probably to

   A. connect the client to a parole officer or drug counselor who can locate an ex-offender or recovered person who might be interviewed first
   B. contact an advocate from a local office who will strenuously promote the client's job applications
   C. instruct the client to avoid mentioning this aspect of his/her history to potential employers, unless asked about it directly
   D. limit job applications to jobs that involve structured, unskilled tasks

20. During a job interview, an interviewer sometimes appears to be imposing periods of silence. Usually, this is because the interviewer

   A. is testing the candidate to see how he reacts to imposed stress
   B. is manifesting her own confidence in the situation
   C. would like the candidate to elaborate on a response
   D. lacks experience and is formulating the next question

21. When using interest inventories in client exploration, counselors should typically be aware of common problems associated with their application. Which of the following is NOT one of these problems?

    A. Scores may produce a very abbreviated list of suggested occupations.
    B. There are few reliable interest inventories that are keyed directly to occupational options.
    C. The objective information produced by the scores often leads to insufficient counseling.
    D. Clients are often inclined to focus attention on interest scores to confirm their own subjective evaluations, and then move their attention to occupations suggested by those scores.

22. Large group instruction is sometimes used in job search or career education, but it has the significant DISADVANTAGE of

    A. requiring credentialed educators
    B. disseminating large amounts of information to numerous individuals at once
    C. absorbing too much of the client's job search responsibilities
    D. not allowing for group interaction or individual clarification of information

23. A newspaper want ad states that an applicant for a position must have 3–5 years experience in the field. Typically, a client should be encouraged to apply if he has

    A. no experience in the field but is willing to learn
    B. less than one year of experience
    C. one year of experience plus other skills
    D. more than 10 years experience in the field

24. The Strong–Campbell Interest Inventory (SCII) is generally considered to be a useful career–planning tool for each of the following types of job seekers EXCEPT those who

    A. are able to identify some of their likes and dislikes
    B. appear to have some understanding of their career potentials
    C. are considering occupations involving college preparation
    D. appear to be personally confused about the direction their lives are taking

25. Which of the following is NOT an advantage associated with the use of programmed or mechanized materials (workbooks or sequenced exercises) as educational media in job counseling?
    They

    A. allow the client to proceed at a personally determined pace
    B. increase feelings of personalization with each client
    C. assist the client in obtaining information and to process that information in a way that logically moves her toward a decision
    D. assure that specific steps are mastered before advancing to later steps

KEY (CORRECT ANSWERS)

1.	C	11.	D
2.	A	12.	D
3.	A	13.	C
4.	C	14.	C
5.	B	15.	D
6.	C	16.	B
7.	C	17.	A
8.	C	18.	B
9.	C	19.	A
10.	D	20.	A

21. B
22. D
23. C
24. D
25. B

EXAMINATION SECTION
TEST 1

DIRECTIONS: Each question or incomplete statement is followed by several suggested answers or completions. Select the one that BEST answers the question or completes the statement. *PRINT THE LETTER OF THE CORRECT ANSWER IN THE SPACE AT THE RIGHT.*

1. One of the major objectives of a pre-employment interview is to get the interviewee to respond freely to inquiries.
   The one of the following actions that would be MOST likely to restrict the conversation of the interviewee would be for the investigator to
   A. keep a stenographic record of the interviewee's statements
   B. ask questions requiring complete explanations
   C. pose direct, specific questions to the interviewee
   D. allow the interviewee to respond to questions at his own pace

2. One of the reasons for the widespread use of the interview in personnel selection is that the interview
   A. has been shown to be a valid measurement technique
   B. is efficient and reliable
   C. has been demonstrated to result in consistency among raters
   D. allows for flexibility of response

3. In conducting a personnel interview, which of the following guidelines would be MOST desirable for the interviewer to follow?
   A. Allocate the same amount of time to each person being interviewed to standardize the process
   B. Ask exactly the same questions of all persons being interviewed to increase the objectivity of the process
   C. Eliminate the use of non-directive techniques because of their subjectivity
   D. Vary his style and technique to fit the purpose of the interview and the people being interviewed

4. You are planning to conduct preliminary interviews of applicants for an important position in your department.
   Which of the following planning considerations is LEAST likely to contribute to successful interviews?
   A. Make provisions to conduct interviews in privacy
   B. Schedule your appointments so that interviews will be short
   C. Prepare a list of your objectives
   D. Learn as much as you can about the applicant before the interview

5. When dealing with an aggrieved worker, a USEFUL interviewing technique is to
   A. maintain a sympathetic attitude
   B. maintain an attitude of cold impartiality

2 (#1)

C. assure the subject that you are on his side
D. display a tape recorder to give the subject confidence that no parts of his story will be overlooked

6. The "patterned interview" is a device used by sophisticated employers to
   A. select employees who fit the ethnic pattern of the community
   B. ascertain the pattern of facts surrounding a grievance
   C. discourage workers from joining unions
   D. appraises a subject's most important character traits

6._____

7. One of the applicants for a menial job is a tall, stooped, husky individual with a low forehead, narrow eyes, a protruding chin, and a tendency to keep his mouth open.
   In interviewing him, you should
   A. check him more carefully than the other applicants regarding criminal background
   B. disregard any skills he might have for other jobs which are vacant
   C. make your vocabulary somewhat simpler than with the other applicants
   D. make no assumptions regarding his ability on the basis of his appearance

7._____

8. Of the following, the BEST approach for you to use at the beginning of an interview with a job applicant is to
   A. caution him to use his time economically and to get to the point
   B. ask him how long he intends to remain on the job if hired
   C. make some pleasant remarks to put him at ease
   D. emphasize the importance of the interview in obtaining the job

8._____

9. Of the following, the BEST reason for conducting an "exit interview" with an employee is to
   A. make certain that he returns all identification cards and office keys
   B. find out why he is leaving
   C. provide a useful training device for the exit interviewer
   D. discover if his initial hiring was in error

9._____

10. If you are to interview several applicants for jobs and rate them on five different factors on a scale of 1 to 5, you should be MOST careful to *insure* that your
    A. rating on one factor does not influence your rating on another factor
    B. ratings on all factors are interrelated with a minimum of variation
    C. overall evaluation for employment exactly reflects the arithmetic average of your ratings
    D. overall evaluation for employment is unrelated to your individual ratings

10._____

11. Of the following, the question MOST appropriate for initial screening purposes GENERALLY is:
    A. What are your salary requirements?
    B. Why do you think you would like this kind of work?
    C. How did you get along with your last supervisor?
    D. What are your vocational goals?

11._____

3 (#1)

12. Of the following, normally the question MOST appropriate for selection purposes generally would tend to be:
    A. Where did you work last?
    B. When did you graduate from high school?
    C. What was your average in school?
    D. Why did you select this organization?

    12.____

13. Assume that you have been asked to interview each of several students who have been hired to work part-time.
    Which of the following would ordinarily be accomplished LEAST effectively in such an interview?
    A. Providing information about the organization or institution in which the students will be working
    B. Directing the students to report for work each afternoon at specified times
    C. Determining experience and background of the students so that appropriate assignments can be made
    D. Changing the attitudes of the students toward the importance of parental controls

    13.____

14. In interviewing job applicants, which of the following usually does NOT have to be done before the end of the interview?
    A. Making a decision to hire an applicant
    B. Securing information from applicants
    C. Giving information to applicants
    D. Establishing a friendly relationship with applicants

    14.____

15. In the process of interviewing applicants for a position on your staff, the one of the following which would be BEST is to
    A. make sure all applicants are introduced to the other members of your staff prior to the formal interview
    B. make sure the applicant does not ask questions about the job or the department
    C. avoid having the applicant talk with the staff at the conclusion of a successful interview
    D. introduce applicants to some of the staff at the conclusion of a successful interview

    15.____

16. While interviewing a job applicant, you ask applicant why he left his last job. The applicant does not answer immediately.
    Of the following, the BEST action to take at that point is to
    A. wait until he answers
    B. ask another question
    C. repeat the question in a loud voice
    D. ask him why he does not answer

    16.____

17. You know that a student applying for a job in your office has done well in college except for two courses in science. However, when you ask him about his grades, his reply is vague and general.

    17.____

It would be BEST for you to
- A. lead the applicant to admitting doing poorly in science to be sure that the facts are correct
- B. judge the applicant's tact and skill in handling what may be for him a personally sensitive question
- C. immediately confront the applicant with the facts and ask for an explanation
- D. ignore the applicant's response since you have the transcript

18. A college student has applied for a position with your department. Prior to conducting an interview of the job applicant, it would be LEAST helpful for you to have
    - A. a personal resume
    - B. a job description
    - C. references
    - D. hiring requirements

19. Job applicants tend to be nervous during interviews. Which of the following techniques is MOST likely to put such an applicant at ease?
    - A. Try to establish rapport by asking general questions which are easily answered by the applicant
    - B. Ask the applicant to describe his career objectives immediately, thus minimizing the anxiety caused by waiting
    - C. Start the interview with another member of the staff present so that the applicant does not feel alone
    - D. Proceed as rapidly as possible, since the emotional state of the applicant is none of your concern

20. At the first interview between a supervisor and a newly appointed subordinate, GREATEST care should be taken to
    - A. build toward a satisfactory personal relationship even if some other objectives of the interview must be postponed
    - B. cover a predetermined list of specific objectives so as to make a further orientation interview unnecessary
    - C. create an image of a forceful, determined supervisor whose wishes cannot be opposed by a subordinate without great risk
    - D. create an impression of efficiency and control of operation free from interpersonal relationships

21. You are a supervisor in an agency and are holding your first interview with a new employee.
    In this interview, you should strive MAINLY to
    - A. show the new employee that you are an efficient and objective supervisor, with a completely impersonal attitude toward your subordinates
    - B. complete the entire orientation process including the giving of detailed job-duty instructions

C. make it clear to the employee that all your decisions are based on your many years of experience
D. lay the groundwork for a good employee-supervisor relationship by gaining the new employee's confidence

22. The INCORRECT statement related to the principles of interviewing is:
    A. Written outlines should be avoided by the interviewer because they tend to be overly restrictive.
    B. Preliminary planning (for the interview) should involve an analysis of the point of view of the person to be interviewed.
    C. An interviewing supervisor should make every effort to conduct it in privacy to avoid possible inhibitions.
    D. Well-planned questions are sometimes necessary in conducting an interview.

23. Assume that you are conducting an interview with a prospective employee who is of limited mental ability and low socio-economic status.
    Of the following, it is MOST likely that asking him many open-ended questions about his work experience would cause him to respond
    A. articulately   B. reluctantly   C. comfortably   D. aggressively

24. An individual interview is to be used as part of an examination for a supervisory position.
    Of the following, the attribute or characteristic that is LEAST suitable for evaluation in such an interview is
    A. ability to supervise people   B. poise and confidence
    C. response to stress conditions   D. rigidity and flexibility

25. In conducting a disciplinary interview, a supervisor finds that he must ask some highly personal questions which are relevant to the problem at hand.
    The interviewer is MOST likely to get TRUTHFUL answers to these questions if he asks them
    A. early in the interview, before the interviewee has had a chance to become emotional
    B. in a manner so that the interviewee can answer them with a simple "yes" or "no"
    C. well into the interview, after rapport and trust have been established
    D. just after the close of the interview, so that the questions appear to be off the record

KEY (CORRECT ANSWERS)

1.	A		11.	A
2.	D		12.	D
3.	D		13.	D
4.	B		14.	A
5.	A		15.	D
6.	D		16.	A
7.	D		17.	B
8.	C		18.	C
9.	B		19.	A
10.	A		20.	A

21. D
22. A
23. B
24. A
25. C

TEST 2

DIRECTIONS: Each question or incomplete statement is followed by several suggested answers or completions. Select the one that BEST answers the question or completes the statement. *PRINT THE LETTER OF THE CORRECT ANSWER IN THE SPACE AT THE RIGHT.*

1. Of the following methods of conducting an interview, the BEST is to
   A. ask questions with "yes" or "no" answers
   B. listen carefully and ask only questions that are pertinent
   C. fire questions at the interviewee so that he must answer sincerely and briefly
   D. read standardized questions to the person being interviewed

   1.____

2. An interviewer should begin with topics which are easy to talk about and which are not threatening.
   This procedure is useful MAINLY because it
   A. allows the applicant a little time to get accustomed to the situation and leads to freer communication
   B. distracts the attention of the person being interviewed from the main purpose of the questioning
   C. is the best way for the interviewer to show that he is relaxed and confident on the job
   D. causes the interviewee to feel that the interviewer is apportioning valuable questioning time

   2.____

3. The initial interview will normally be more of a problem to the interviewer than any subsequent interviews he may have with the same person because
   A. the interviewee is likely to be hostile
   B. there is too much to be accomplished in one session
   C. he has less information about the client than he will have later
   D. some information may be forgotten when later making record of this first interview

   3.____

4. Most successful interviews are those in which the interviewer shows a genuine interest in the person he is questioning.
   This attitude would MOST likely cause the individual being interviewed to
   A. feel that the interviewer already knows all the facts in his case
   B. act more naturally and reveal more of his true feelings
   C. request that the interviewer give more attention to his problems, not his personality
   D. react defensively, suppress his negative feelings and conceal the real facts in his case

   4.____

5. When interviewing a person, the interviewer may easily slip into error in rating his subject's personal qualities because of the general impression he receives of the individual.
   This tendency is known as the
   A. "halo" effect
   B. subjective bias problem
   C. "person-to-person" error
   D. inflation effect

   5.____

6. An interviewer would find an interview checklist LEAST useful for
   A. making sure that all the principal facts are secured in the interview
   B. insuring that the claimant's grievance is settled in his favor
   C. facilitating later research into the nature of the problems handled by the agency
   D. conducting the interview in a logical and orderly fashion

7. There are almost as many techniques of interviewing as there are interviews. Of the following, the LEAST objectionable method is to
   A. ask if interviewee minds being quoted
   B. make occasional notes as important topics some up
   C. take notes unobtrusively
   D. take shorthand notes of every word

8. Questions worded so that the person being interviewed has some hint of the desired answer can modify the person's response.
   The result of the inclusion of such questions in an interview, even when they ae used inadvertently, is to
   A. have no effect on the basic content of the information given by the person interviewed
   B. have value in convincing the person that the suggested plan is the best for him
   C. cause the person to give more meaningful information
   D. reduce the validity of the meaningful information obtained from the person

9. The person MOST likely to be a good interviewer is one who
   A. is able to outguess the person being interviewed
   B. tries to change the attitudes of the persons he interviews
   C. controls the interview by skillfully dominating the conversation
   D. is able to imagine himself in the position of the person being interviewed

10. The "halo effect" is an overall impression on the interviewee, whether favorable or unfavorable, usually created by a single trait. This impression then influences the appraisal of all other factors.
    A "halo effect" is LEAST likely to be created at an interview where the interviewee is a
    A. person of average appearance and ability
    B. rough-looking man who uses abusive language
    C. young attractive woman being interviewed by a man
    D. person who demonstrates an exceptional ability to remember faces

11. Of the following, the BEST way for an interviewer to calm a person who seems to have become emotionally upset as a result of a question asked is for the interviewer to
    A. talk to the person about other things for a short time
    B. ask that the person control himself
    C. probe for the cause of his emotional upset
    D. finish the questioning as quickly as possible

12. Of the following, the GREATEST pitfall in interviewing is that the result may be affected by the
    A. bias of the interviewee
    B. bias of the interviewer
    C. educational level of the interviewee
    D. educational level of the interviewer

13. Assume you are assigned to interview applicants.
    Of the following, which is the BEST attitude for you to take in dealing with applicants?
    A. Assume they will enjoy being interviewed because they believe that you have the power of decision
    B. Expect that they have a history of anti-social behavior in the family, and probe deeply into the social development of family members
    C. Expect that they will try to control the interview, thus you should keep them on the defensive
    D. Assume that they will be polite and cooperative and attempt to secure the information you need in a business-like manner

14. A Spanish-speaking applicant may want to bring his bilingual child with him to an interview to act as an interpreter.
    Which of the following would be LEAST likely to affect the value of an interview in which an applicant's child has acted as interpreter?
    A. It may make it undesirable to ask certain questions.
    B. A child may do an inadequate job of interpretation.
    C. A child's answers may indicate his feelings toward his parents.
    D. The applicant may not want to reveal all information in front of his child.

15. In answering questions asked by students, faculty, and the public, it is MOST important that
    A. you indicate your source of information
    B. you are not held responsible for the answers
    C. the facts you give be accurate
    D. the answers cover every possible aspect of each question

16. Assume that someone you are interviewing is reluctant to give you certain information.
    He would probably be MORE responsive if you show him that
    A. all the other persons you interviewed provided you with the information
    B. it would serve his own best interests to give you the information
    C. the information is very important to you
    D. you are business-like and take a no-nonsense approach

17. Taking notes while you are interviewing someone is MOST likely to
    A. arouse doubts as to your trustworthiness
    B. give the interviewee confidence in your ability
    C. insure that you record the facts you think are important
    D. make the responses of the interviewee unreliable

18. In developing a role-playing situation to be used to train interviewers, the one of the following that it would be MOST important to use as a guide is that the situation
    A. allow the role player to identify readily with the role he is to play
    B. be free of actual or potential conflict between the role players
    C. can be clearly recognized by the participants as an actual interview situation that has already taken place
    D. should provide a detailed set of specifications for handling the roles to be played

19. Restating a question before the person being interviewed gives an answer to the original question is usually NOT good practice principally because
    A. the client will think that you don't know your job
    B. it may confuse the client
    C. the interviewer should know exactly what to ask and how to put the question
    D. it reveals the interviewer's insecurity

20. In interviewing a man who has a grievance, it is IMPORTANT that the interviewer
    A. take note of such physical responses as shifty eyes
    B. use a lie detector, if possible, to ascertain the truth in doubtful situations
    C. allow the complainant to "tell his story"
    D. place the complainant under oath

21. Ideally, the setting for an interview should NOT include
    A. an informal opening   B. privacy and comfort
    C. an atmosphere of leisure   D. a lie detector

22. Which of the following is an example of a "non-directive" interview?
    A. The subject directs his remarks at someone other than the interviewer.
    B. The subject discusses any topics that seem to be relevant to him.
    C. The subject has not been directed that he need answer any particular questions.
    D. The interview is confined to the facts of the case and is not directed at eliciting personal information.

23. Of the following abilities, the one which is LEAST important in conducting an interview is the ability to
    A. ask the interviewee pertinent questions
    B. evaluate the interviewee on the basis of appearance
    C. evaluate the responses of the interviewee
    D. gain the cooperation of the interviewee

24. Which of the following actions would be LEAST desirable for you to take when you have to conduct an interview? 24.____
    A. Set a relaxed and friendly atmosphere
    B. Plan your interview ahead of time
    C. Allow the person interviewed to structure the interview as he wishes
    D. Include some stock or standard question which you ask everyone.

25. One of the MOST important techniques for conducting good interviews is 25.____
    A. asking the applicant questions in rapid succession, thereby keeping the conversation properly focused
    B. listening carefully to all that the applicant has to say, making mental notes of possible areas for follow-up
    C. indicating to the applicant the criteria and standards on which you will base your judgment
    D. making sure that you are interrupted about five minutes before you wish to end so that you can keep on schedule

KEY (CORRECT ANSWERS)

1.	B		11.	A
2.	A		12.	B
3.	C		13.	D
4.	B		14.	C
5.	A		15.	C
6.	B		16.	B
7.	C		17.	C
8.	D		18.	A
9.	D		19.	B
10.	A		20.	C

21. D
22. B
23. B
24. C
25. B

PREPARING WRITTEN MATERIALS
EXAMINATION SECTION
TEST 1

DIRECTIONS: Each question consists of a sentence which may be classified appropriately under one of the following four categories:
- A. Incorrect because of faulty grammar or sentence structure.
- B. Incorrect because of faulty punctuation.
- C. Incorrect because of faulty spelling or capitalization.
- D. Correct

Examine each sentence carefully. Then, in the space at the right, print the capital letter preceding the option which is the BEST of the four suggested above. All incorrect sentences contain only one type of error. Consider a sentence correct if it contains none of the types of errors mentioned, although there may be other correct ways of expressing the same thought.

1. The fire apparently started in the storeroom, which is usually locked. 1.____

2. On approaching the victim two bruises were noticed by this officer. 2.____

3. The officer, who was there examined the report with great care. 3.____

4. Each employee in the office had a separate desk. 4.____

5. The suggested procedure is similar to the one now in use. 5.____

6. No one was more pleased with the new procedure than the chauffeur. 6.____

7. He tried to pursuade her to change the procedure. 7.____

8. The total of the expenses charged to petty cash were high. 8.____

9. An understanding between him and I was finally reached. 9.____

10. It was at the supervisor's request that the clerk agreed to postpone his vacation. 10.____

11. We do not believe that it is necessary for both he and the clerk to attend the conference. 11.____

12. All employees, who display perseverance, will be given adequate recognition. 12.____

13. He regrets that some of us employees are dissatisfied with our new assignments. 13.____

14. "Do you think that the raise was merited," asked the supervisor?   14.____

15. The new manual of procedure is a valuable supplament to our rules and   15.____
    regulation.

16. The typist admitted that she had attempted to pursuade the other employees   16.____
    to assist her in her work.

17. The supervisor asked that all amendments to the regulations be handled by   17.____
    you and I.

18. They told both he and I that the prisoner had escaped.   18.____

19. Any superior officer, who, disregards the just complaints of his subordinates, 19.____
    is remiss in the performance of his duty.

20. Only those members of the national organization who resided in the Middle   20.____
    west attended the conference in Chicago.

21. We told him to give the investigation assignment to whoever was available.   21.____

22. Please do not disappoint and embarass us by not appearing in court.   22.____

23. Despite the efforts of the Supervising mechanic, the elevator could not be   23.____
    started.

24. The U.S. Weather Bureau, weather record for the accident date was checked.   24.____

KEY (CORRECT ANSWERS)

1.	D		11.	A
2.	A		12.	B
3.	B		13.	D
4.	D		14.	B
5.	D		15.	C
6.	D		16.	C
7.	C		17.	A
8.	A		18.	A
9.	A		19.	B
10.	D		20.	C

21. D
22. C
23. C
24. B

TEST 2

DIRECTIONS: Each question consists of a sentence. Some of the sentences contain errors in English grammar or usage, punctuation, spelling, or capitalization. A sentence does not contain an error simply because it could be written in a different manner. Choose answer:
- A. If the sentence contains an error in English grammar or usage.
- B. if the sentence contains an error in punctuation.
- C. If the sentence contains an error in spelling or capitalization
- D. If the sentence does not contain any errors.

1. The severity of the sentence prescribed by contemporary statutes—including both the former and the revised New York Penal Laws—do not depend on what crime was intended by the offender.   1.____

2. It is generally recognized that two defects in the early law of attempt played a part in the birth of burglary: (1) immunity from prosecution for conduct short of the last act before completion of the crime, and (2) the relatively minor penalty imposed for an attempt (it being a common law misdemeanor) vis-à-vis the completed offense.   2.____

3. The first sentence of the statute is applicable to employees who enter their place of employment, invited guests, and all other persons who have an express or implied license or privilege to enter the premises.   3.____

4. Contemporary criminal codes in the United States generally divide burglary into various degrees, differentiating the categories according to place, time and other attendent circumstances.   4.____

5. The assignment was completed in record time but the payroll for it has not yet been prepaid.   5.____

6. The operator, on the other hand, is willing to learn me how to use the mimeograph.   6.____

7. She is the prettiest of the three sisters.   7.____

8. She doesn't know; if the mail has arrived.   8.____

9. The doorknob of the office door is broke.   9.____

10. Although the department's supply of scratch pads and stationery have diminished considerably, the allotment for our division has not been reduced.   10.____

11. You have not told us whom you wish to designate as your secretary.   11.____

12. Upon reading the minutes of the last meeting, the new proposal was taken up for consideration.   12.____

13. Before beginning the discussion, we locked the door as a precautionery measure.   13.____

14. The supervisor remarked, "Only those clerks, who perform routine work, are permitted to take a rest period."   14.____

15. Not only will this duplicating machine make accurate copies, but it will also produce a quantity of work equal to fifteen transcribing typists.   15.____

16. "Mr. Jones," said the supervisor, "we regret our inability to grant you an extention of your leave of absence."   16.____

17. Although the employees find the work monotonous and fatigueing, they rarely complain.   17.____

18. We completed the tabulation of the receipts on time despite the fact that Miss Smith our fastest operator was absent for over a week.   18.____

19. The reaction of the employees who attended the meeting, as well as the reaction of those who did not attend, indicates clearly that the schedule is satisfactory to everyone concerned.   19.____

20. Of the two employees, the one in our office is the most efficient.   20.____

21. No one can apply or even understand, the new rules and regulations.   21.____

22. A large amount of supplies were stored in the empty office.   22.____

23. If an employee is occassionally asked to work overtime, he should do so willingly.   23.____

24. It is true that the new procedures are difficult to use but, we are certain that you will learn them quickly.   24.____

25. The office manager said that he did not know who would be given a large allotment under the new plan.   25.____

KEY (CORRECT ANSWERS)

1.	A	11.	D
2.	D	12.	A
3.	D	13.	C
4.	C	14.	B
5.	C	15.	A
6.	A	16.	C
7.	D	17.	C
8.	B	18.	B
9.	A	19.	D
10.	A	20.	A

21. B
22. A
23. C
24. B
25. D

TEST 3

DIRECTIONS: Each of the following sentences may be classified MOST appropriately under one of the following categories:
  A. Faulty because of incorrect grammar
  B. Faulty because of incorrect punctuation
  C. Faulty because of incorrect capitalization
  D. Correct

Examine each sentence carefully. Then, in the space at the right, print the capital letter preceding the option which is the BEST of the four suggested above. All incorrect sentence contain but one type of error. Consider a sentence correct if it contains none of the types of errors mentioned, even though there may be other correct ways of expressing the same thought.

1. The desk, as well as the chairs, were moved out of the office. 1.____

2. The clerk whose production was greatest for the month won a day's vacation as first prize. 2.____

3. Upon entering the room, the employees were found hard at work at their desks. 3.____

4. John Smith our new employee always arrives at work on time. 4.____

5. Punish whoever is guilty of stealing the money. 5.____

6. Intelligent and persistent effort lead to success no matter what the job may be. 6.____

7. The secretary asked, "can you call again at three o'clock?" 7.____

8. He told us, that if the report was not accepted at the next meeting, it would have to be rewritten. 8.____

9. He would not have sent the letter if he had known that it would cause so much excitement. 9.____

10. We all looked forward to him coming to visit us. 10.____

11. If you find that you are unable to complete the assignment please notify me as soon as possible. 11.____

12. Every girl in the office went home on time but me; there was still some work for me to finish. 12.____

13. He wanted to know who the letter was addressed to, Mr. Brown or Mr. Smith. 13.____

14. "Mr. Jones, he said, please answer this letter as soon as possible." 14.____

15. The new clerk had an unusual accent inasmuch as he was born and educated in the south. 15._____

16. Although he is younger than her, he earns a higher salary. 16._____

17. Neither of the two administrators are going to attend the conference being held in Washington, D.C. 17._____

18. Since Miss Smith and Miss Jones have more experience than us, they have been given more responsible duties. 18._____

19. Mr. Shaw the supervisor of the stock room maintains an inventory of stationery and office supplies. 19._____

20. Inasmuch as this matter affects both you and I, we should take joint action. 20._____

21. Who do you think will be able to perform this highly technical work? 21._____

22. Of the two employees, John is considered the most competent. 22._____

23. He is not coming home on tuesday; we expect him next week. 23._____

24. Stenographers, as well as typists must be able to type rapidly and accurately. 24._____

25. Having been placed in the safe we were sure that the money would not be stolen. 25._____

KEY (CORRECT ANSWERS)

1.	A		11.	B
2.	D		12.	D
3.	A		13.	A
4.	B		14.	B
5.	D		15.	C
6.	A		16.	A
7.	C		17.	A
8.	B		18.	A
9.	D		19.	B
10.	A		20.	A

21. D
22. A
23. C
24. B
25. A

TEST 4

DIRECTIONS: Each of the following sentences consist of four sentences lettered A, B, C, and D. One of the sentences in each group contains an error in grammar or punctuation. Indicate the INCORRECT sentence in each group. *PRINT THE LETTER OF THE CORRECT ANSWER IN THE SPACE AT THE RIGHT.*

1. A. Give the message to whoever is on duty. 1.____
   B. The teacher who's pupil won first prize presented the award.
   C. Between you and me, I don't expect the program to succeed.
   D. His running to catch the bus caused the accident.

2. A. The process, which was patented only last year is already obsolete. 2.____
   B. His interest in science (which continues to the present) led him to convert his basement into a laboratory.
   C. He described the book as "verbose, repetitious, and bombastic".
   D. Our new director will need to possess three qualities: vision, patience, and fortitude.

3. A. The length of ladder trucks varies considerably. 3.____
   B. The probationary fireman reported to the officer to who he was assigned.
   C. The lecturer emphasized the need for we firemen to be punctual.
   D. Neither the officers nor the members of the company knew about the new procedure.

4. A. Ham and eggs is the specialty of the house. 4.____
   B. He is one of the students who are on probation.
   C. Do you think that either one of us have a chance to be nominated for president of the class?
   D. I assume that either he was to be in charge or you were.

5. A. Its a long road that has no turn. 5.____
   B. To run is more tiring than to walk.
   C. We have been assigned three new reports: namely, the statistical summary, the narrative summary, and the budgetary summary.
   D. Had the first payment been made in January, the second would be due in April.

6. A. Each employer has his own responsibilities. 6.____
   B. If a person speaks correctly, they make a good impression.
   C. Every one of the operators has had her vacation.
   D. Has anybody filed his report?

7. A. The manager, with all his salesmen, was obliged to go. 7.____
   B. Who besides them is to sign the agreement?
   C. One report without the others is incomplete.
   D. Several clerks, as well as the proprietor, was injured.

2 (#4)

8. A. A suspension of these activities is expected.
    B. The machine is economical because first cost and upkeep are low.
    C. A knowledge of stenography and filing are required for this position.
    D. The condition in which the goods were received shows that the packing was not done properly.

8._____

9. A. There seems to be a great many reasons for disagreement.
    B. It does not seem possible that they could have failed.
    C. Have there always been too few applicants for these positions?
    D. There is no excuse for these errors.

9._____

10. A. We shall be pleased to answer your question.
    B. Shall we plan the meeting for Saturday?
    C. I will call you promptly at seven.
    D. Can I borrow your book after you have read it?

10._____

11. A. You are as capable as I.
    B. Everyone is willing to sign but him and me.
    C. As for he and his assistant, I cannot praise them too highly.
    D. Between you and me, I think he will be dismissed.

11._____

12. A. Our competitors bid above us last week.
    B. The survey which was began last year has not yet been completed.
    C. The operators had shown that they understood their instructions.
    D. We have never ridden over worse roads.

12._____

13. A. Who did they say was responsible?
    B. Whom did you suspect?
    C. Who do you suppose it was?
    D. Whom do you mean?

13._____

14. A. Of the two propositions, this is the worse.
    B. Which report do you consider the best—the one in January or the one in July?
    C. I believe this is the most practicable of the many plans submitted.
    D. He is the youngest employee in the organization.

14._____

15. A. The firm had but three orders last week.
    B. That doesn't really seem possible.
    C. After twenty years scarcely none of the old business remains.
    D. Has he done nothing about it?

15._____

KEY (CORRECT ANSWERS)

1.	B	6.	B	11.	C
2.	A	7.	D	12.	B
3.	C	8.	C	13.	A
4.	C	9.	A	14.	B
5.	A	10.	D	15.	C

PREPARING WRITTEN MATERIAL
EXAMINATION SECTION
TEST 1

DIRECTIONS: Each question consists of a sentence which may or may not be an example of good English usage. Examine each sentence, considering grammar, punctuation, spelling, capitalization, and awkwardness. Then choose the correct statement about it from the four choices below it. If the English usage in the sentence given is better than any of the changes suggested in choices B, C, or D, pick choice A. (Do not pick a choice that will change the meaning of the sentence.) *PRINT THE LETTER OF THE CORRECT ANSWER IN THE SPACE AT THE RIGHT.*

1. We attended a staff conference on Wednesday the new safety and fire rules were discussed. 1.____
    A. This is an example of acceptable writing.
    B. The words "safety," "fire," and "rules" should begin with capital letters.
    C. There should be a comma after the word "Wednesday."
    D. There should be a period after the word "Wednesday" and the word "the" should begin with a capital letter.

2. Neither the dictionary or the telephone directory could be found in the office library. 2.____
    A. This is an example of acceptable writing.
    B. The word "or" should be changed to "nor."
    C. The word "library" should be spelled "libery."
    D. The word "neither" should be changed to "either."

3. The report would have been typed correctly if the typist could read the draft. 3.____
    A. This is an example of acceptable writing.
    B. The word "would" should be removed.
    C. The word "have" should be inserted after the word "could."
    D. The word "correctly" should be changed to "correct."

4. The supervisor brought the reports and forms to an employees desk. 4.____
    A. This is an example of acceptable writing.
    B. The word "brought" should be changed to "took."
    C. There should be a comma after the word "reports" and a comma after the word "forms."
    D. The word "employees" should be spelled "employee's."

5. It's important for all the office personnel to submit their vacation schedules on time. 5.____
    A. This is an example of acceptable writing.
    B. The word "It's" should be spelled "Its."
    C. The word "their" should be spelled "they're."
    D. The word "personnel" should be spelled "personal."

81

6. The report, along with the accompanying documents, were submitted for review.
   A. This is an example of acceptable writing.
   B. The words "were submitted" should be changed to "was submitted."
   C. The word "accompanying" should be spelled "accompaning."
   D. The comma after the word "report" should be taken out.

7. If others must use your files, be certain that they understand how the system works, but insist that you do all the filing and refiling.
   A. This is an example of acceptable writing.
   B. There should be a period after the word "works," and the word "but" should start a new sentence.
   C. The words "filing" and "refiling" should be spelled "fileing" and "refileing."
   D. There should be a comma after the word "but."

8. The appeal was not considered because of its late arrival.
   A. This is an example of acceptable writing.
   B. The word "its" should be changed to "it's."
   C. The word "its" should be changed to "the."
   D. The words "late arrival" should be changed to "arrival late."

9. The letter must be read carefuly to determine under which subject it should be filed.
   A. This is an example of acceptable writing.
   B. The word "under" should be changed to "at."
   C. The word "determine" should be spelled "determin."
   D. The word "carefuly" should be spelled "carefully."

10. He showed potential as an office manager, but he lacked skill in delegating work.
    A. This is an example of acceptable writing.
    B. The word "delegating" should be spelled "delagating."
    C. The word "potential" should be spelled "potencial."
    D. The words "he lacked" should be changed to "was lacking."

KEY (CORRECT ANSWERS)

1.	D	6.	B
2.	B	7.	A
3.	C	8.	A
4.	D	9.	D
5.	A	10.	A

TEST 2

DIRECTIONS: Each question consists of a sentence which may or may not be an example of good English usage. Examine each sentence, considering grammar, punctuation, spelling, capitalization, and awkwardness. Then choose the correct statement about it from the four choices below it. If the English usage in the sentence given is better than any of the changes suggested in choices B, C, or D, pick choice A. (Do not pick a choice that will change the meaning of the sentence.) *PRINT THE LETTER OF THE CORRECT ANSWER IN THE SPACE AT THE RIGHT.*

1. The supervisor wants that all staff members report to the office at 9:00 A.M.   1.____
   A. This is an example of acceptable writing.
   B. The word "that" should be removed and the word "to" should be inserted after the word "members."
   C. There should be a comma after the word "wants" and a comma after the word "office."
   D. The word "wants" should be changed to "want" and the word "shall" should be inserted after the word "members."

2. Every morning the clerk opens the office mail and distributes it.   2.____
   A. This is an example of acceptable writing.
   B. The word "opens" should be changed to "open."
   C. The word "mail" should be changed to "letters."
   D. The word "it" should be changed to "them."

3. The secretary typed more fast on a desktop computer than on a laptop computer.   3.____
   A. This is an example of acceptable writing.
   B. The words "more fast" should be changed to "faster."
   C. There should be a comma after the words "desktop computer."
   D. The word "than" should be changed to "then."

4. The new stenographer needed a desk a computer, a chair and a blotter.   4.____
   A. This is an example of acceptable writing.
   B. The word "blotter" should be spelled "blodder."
   C. The word "stenographer" should begin with a capital letter.
   D. There should be a comma after the word "desk."

5. The recruiting officer said, "There are many different goverment jobs available."   5.____
   A. This is an example of acceptable writing.
   B. The word "There" should not be capitalized.
   C. The word "government" should be spelled "government."
   D. The comma after the word "said" should be removed.

6. He can recommend a mechanic whose work is reliable.   6.____
   A. This is an example of acceptable writing.
   B. The word "reliable" should be spelled "relyable."
   C. The word "whose" should be spelled "who's."
   D. The word "mechanic should be spelled "mecanic."

83

7. She typed quickly; like someone who had not a moment to lose. 7.____
    A. This is an example of acceptable writing.
    B. The word "not" should be removed.
    C. The semicolon should be changed to a comma.
    D. The word "quickly" should be placed before instead of after the word "typed."

8. She insisted that she had to much work to do. 8.____
    A. This is an example of acceptable writing.
    B. The word "insisted" should be spelled "incisted."
    C. The word "to" used in front of "much" should be spelled "too."
    D. The word "do" should be changed to "be done."

9. He excepted praise from his supervisor for a job well done. 9.____
    A. This is an example of acceptable writing.
    B. The word "excepted" should be spelled "accepted."
    C. The order of the words "well done" should be changed to "done well."
    D. There should be a comma after the word "supervisor."

10. What appears to be intentional errors in grammar occur several times in the passage. 10.____
    A. This is an example of acceptable writing.
    B. The word "occur" should be spelled "occurr."
    C. The word "appears" should be changed to "appear."
    D. The phrase "several times" should be changed to "from time to time."

KEY (CORRECT ANSWERS)

1.	B	6.	A
2.	A	7.	C
3.	B	8.	C
4.	D	9.	B
5.	C	10.	C

TEST 3

DIRECTIONS: Each question consists of a sentence which may or may not be an example of good English usage. Examine each sentence, considering grammar, punctuation, spelling, capitalization, and awkwardness. Then choose the correct statement about it from the four choices below it. If the English usage in the sentence given is better than any of the changes suggested in choices B, C, or D, pick choice A. (Do not pick a choice that will change the meaning of the sentence.) *PRINT THE LETTER OF THE CORRECT ANSWER IN THE SPACE AT THE RIGHT.*

1. The clerk could have completed the assignment on time if he knows where these materials were located.
    A. This is an example of acceptable writing.
    B. The word "knows" should be replaced by "had known."
    C. The word "were" should be replaced by "had been."
    D. The words "where these materials were located" should be replaced by "the location of these materials."

2. All employees should be given safety training. Not just those who accidents.
    A. This is an example of acceptable writing.
    B. The period after the word "training" should be changed to a colon.
    C. The period after the word "training" should be changed to a semicolon, and the first letter of the word "Not" should be changed to a small "n."
    D. The period after the word "training" should be changed to a comma, and the first letter of the word "Not" should be changed to a small "n."

3. This proposal is designed to promote employee awareness of the suggestion program, to encourage employee participation in the program, and to increase the number of suggestions submitted.
    A. This is an example of acceptable writing.
    B. The word "proposal" should be spelled "proposal."
    C. The words "to increase the number of suggestions submitted" should be changed to "an increase in the number of suggestions is expected."
    D. The word "promote" should be changed to "enhance" and the word "increase" should be changed to "add to."

4. The introduction of inovative managerial techniques should be preceded by careful analysis of the specific circumstances and conditions in each department.
    A. This is an example of acceptable writing.
    B. The word "technique" should be spelled "techneques."
    C. The word "inovative" should be spelled "innovative."
    D. A comma should be placed after the word "circumstances" and after the word "conditions."

5. This occurrence indicates that such criticism embarrasses him.
   A. This is an example of acceptable writing.
   B. The word "occurrence" should be spelled "occurence."
   C. The word "criticism" should be spelled "critisism."
   D. The word "embarrasses" should be spelled "embarasses."

KEY (CORRECT ANSWERS)

1. B
2. D
3. A
4. C
5. A

EXAMINATION SECTION
TEST 1

DIRECTIONS: In each of the following questions, only one of the four sentences conforms to standards of correct usage. The other three contain errors in grammar, diction, or punctuation. Select the choice in each question which BEST conforms to standards of correct usage. Consider a choice correct if it contains none of the errors mentioned above, even though there may be other ways of expressing the same thought. *PRINT THE LETTER OF THE CORRECT ANSWER IN THE SPACE AT THE RIGHT.*

1. A. Because he was ill was no excuse for his behavior
    B. I insist that he see a lawyer before he goes to trial.
    C. He said "that he had not intended to go."
    D. He wasn't out of the office only three days.

    1._____

2. A. He came to the station and pays a porter to carry his bags into the train.
    B. I should have liked to live in medieval times.
    C. My father was born in Linville. A little country town where everybody knows everyone else.
    D. The car, which is parked across the street, is disabled.

    2._____

3. A. He asked the desk clerk for a clean, quiet, room.
    B. I expected James to be lonesome and that he would want to go home.
    C. I have stopped worrying because I have heard nothing further on the subject.
    D. If the board of directors controls the company, they may take actions which are disapproved by the stockholders.

    3._____

4. A. Each of the players knew their place.
    B. He whom you saw on the stage is the son of an actor.
    C. Susan is the smartest of the twin sisters.
    D. Who ever thought of him winning both prizes?

    4._____

5. A. An outstanding trait of early man was their reliance on omens.
    B. Because I had never been there before.
    C. Neither Mr. Jones nor Mr. Smith has completed his work.
    D. While eating my dinner, a dog came to the window.

    5._____

6. A. A copy of the lease, in addition to the Rules and Regulations, are to be given to each tenant.
    B. The Rules and Regulations and a copy of the lease is being given to each tenant.
    C. A copy of the lease, in addition to the Rules and Regulations, is to be given to each tenant.
    D. A copy of the lease, in addition to the Rules and Regulations, are being given to each tenant.

    6._____

2 (#1)

7. A. Although we understood that for him music was a passion, we were disturbed by the fact that he was addicted to sing along with the soloists.
    B. Do you believe that Steven is liable to win a scholarship?
    C. Give the picture to whomever is a connoisseur of art.
    D. Whom do you believe to be the most efficient worker in the office?

7.____

8. A. Each adult who is sure they know all the answers will some day realize their mistake.
    B. Even the most hardhearted villain would have to feel bad about so horrible a tragedy.
    C. Neither being licensed teachers, both aspirants had to pass rigorous tests before being appointed.
    D. The principal reason why he wanted to be designated was because he had never before been to a convention.

8.____

9. A. Being that the weather was so inclement, the party has been postponed for at least a month.
    B. He is in New York City only three weeks and he has already seen all the thrilling sights in Manhattan and in the other four boroughs.
    C. If you will look it up in the official directory, which can be consulted in the library during specified hours, you will discover that the chairman and director are Mr. T. Henry Long.
    D. Working hard at college during the day and at the post office during the night, he appeared to his family to be indefatigable.

9.____

10. A. I would have been happy to oblige you if you only asked me to do it.
    B. The cold weather, as well as the unceasing wind and rain, have made us decide to spend the winter in Florida.
    C. The politician would have been more successful in winning office if he would have been less dogmatic.
    D. These trousers are expensive; however, they will wear well.

10.____

11. A. All except him wore formal attire at the reception for the ambassador.
    B. If that chair were to be blown off of the balcony, it might injure someone below.
    C. Not a passenger, who was in the crash, survived the impact.
    D. To borrow money off friends is the best way to lose them.

11.____

12. A. Approaching Manhattan on the ferry boat from Staten Island, an unforgettable sight of the skyscrapers is seen.
    B. Did you see the exhibit of modernistic paintings as yet?
    C. Gesticulating wildly and ranting in stentorian tones, the speaker was the sinecure of all eyes.
    D. The airplane with crew and passengers was lost somewhere in the Pacific Ocean.

12.____

3 (#1)

13. A. If one has consistently had that kind of training, it is certainly too late to change your entire method of swimming long distances.
    B. The captain would have been more impressed if you would have been more conscientious in evacuation drills.
    C. The passengers on the stricken ship were all ready to abandon it at the signal.
    D. The villainous shark lashed at the lifeboat with it's tail, trying to upset the rocking boat in order to partake of it's contents.

13.____

14. A. As one whose been certified as a professional engineer, I believe that the decision to build a bridge over that harbor is unsound.
    B. Between you and me, this project ought to be completed long before winter arrives.
    C. He fervently hoped that the men would be back at camp and to find them busy at their usual chores.
    D. Much to his surprise, he discovered that the climate of Korea was like his home town.

14.____

15. A. An industrious executive is aided, not impeded, by having a hobby which gives him a fresh point of view on life and its problems.
    B. Frequent absence during the calendar year will surely mitigate against the chances of promotion.
    C. He was unable to go to the committee meeting because he was very ill.
    D. Mr. Brown expressed his disapproval so emphatically that his associates were embarassed

15.____

16. A. At our next session, the office manager will have told you something about his duties and responsibilities.
    B. In general, the book is absorbing and original and have no hesitation about recommending it.
    C. The procedures followed by private industry in dealing with lateness and absence are different from ours.
    D We shall treat confidentially any information about Mr. Doe, to whom we understand you have sent reports to for many years.

16.____

17. A. I talked to one official, whom I knew was fully impartial.
    B. Everyone signed the petition but him.
    C. He proved not only to be a good student but also a good athlete.
    D. All are incorrect.

17.____

18. A. Every year a large amount of tenants are admitted to housing projects.
    B. Henry Ford owned around a billion dollars in industrial equipment.
    C. He was aggravated by the child's poor behavior.
    D. All are incorrect.

18.____

19. A. Before he was committed to the asylum he suffered from the illusion that 19.____
       he was Napoleon.
    B. Besides stocks, there were also bonds in the safe.
    C. We bet the other team easily.
    D. All are incorrect.

20. A. Bring this report to your supervisory. 20.____
    B. He set the chair down near the table.
    C. The capitol of New York is Albany.
    D. All are incorrect.

21. A. He was chosen to arbitrate the dispute because everyone knew he would 21.____
       be disinterested.
    B. It is advisable to obtain the best council before making an important
       decision.
    C. Less college students are interested in teaching than ever before.
    D. All are incorrect.

22. A. She, hearing a signal, the source lamp flashed. 22.____
    B. While hearing a signal, the source lamp flashed.
    C. In hearing a signal, the source lamp flashed.
    D. As she heard a signal, the source lamp flashed.

23. A. Every one of the time records have been initialed in the designated spaces. 23.____
    B. All of the time records has been initialed in the designated spaces.
    C. Each one of the time records was initialed in the designated spaces.
    D. The time records all been initialed in the designated spaces.

24. A. If there is no one else to answer the phone, you will have to answer it. 24.____
    B. You will have to answer it yourself if no one else answers the phone.
    C. If no one else is not around to pick up the phone, you will have to do it.
    D. You will have to answer the phone when nobodys here to do it.

25. A. Dr. Barnes not in his office. What could I do for you? 25.____
    B. Dr. Barnes is not in his office. Is there something I can do for you?
    C. Since Dr. Barnes is not in his office, might there be something I may do for
       you?
    D. Is there any ways I can assist you since Dr. Barnes is not in his office?

26. A. She do not understand how the new console works. 26.____
    B. The way the new console works, she doesn't understand.
    C. She doesn't understand how the new console works.
    D. The new console works, so that she doesn't understand.

27. A. Certain changes in my family income must be reported as they occur. 27.____
    B. When certain changes in family income occur, it must be reported.
    C. Certain family income change must be reported as they occur.
    D. Certain changes in family income must be reported as they have been
       occurring.

28. A. Each tenant has to complete the application themselves.
    B. Each of the tenants have to complete the application by himself.
    C. Each of the tenants has to complete the application himself.
    D. Each of the tenants has to complete the application by themselves.

28.____

29. A. Yours is the only building that the construction will effect.
    B. Your's is the only building affected by the construction.
    C. The construction will only effect your building.
    D. Yours is the only building that will be affected by the construction.

29.____

30. A. There is four tests left.
    B. The number of tests left are four.
    C. There are four tests left.
    D. Four of the tests remains.

30.____

31. A. Each of the applicants takes a test.
    B. Each of the applicant take a test.
    C. Each of the applicants take tests.
    D. Each of the applicants have taken tests.

31.____

32. A. The applicant, not the examiners, are ready.
    B. The applicants, not the examiners, is ready.
    C. The applicants, not the examiner, are ready.
    D. The applicant, not the examiner, are ready

32.____

33. A. You will not progress except you practice.
    B. You will not progress without you practicing.
    C. You will not progress unless you practice.
    D. You will not progress provided you do not practice.

33.____

34. A. Neither the director or the employees will be at the office tomorrow.
    B. Neither the director nor the employees will be at the office tomorrow.
    C. Neither the director, or the secretary nor the other employees will be at the office tomorrow.
    D. Neither the director, the secretary or the other employees will be at the office tomorrow.

34.____

35. A. In my absence, he and her will have to finish the assignment.
    B. In my absence he and she will have to finish the assignment.
    C. In my absence she and him, they will have to finish the assignment.
    D. In my absence he and her both will have to finish the assignment.

35.____

KEY (CORRECT ANSWERS)

1.	B	11.	A	21.	A	31.	A
2.	B	12.	D	22.	D	32.	C
3.	C	13.	C	23.	C	33.	C
4.	B	14.	B	24.	A	34.	B
5.	C	15.	A	25.	B	35.	B
6.	C	16.	C	26.	C		
7.	D	17.	B	27.	A		
8.	B	18.	D	28.	C		
9.	D	19.	B	29.	D		
10.	D	20.	B	30.	C		

TEST 2

DIRECTIONS: Each question or incomplete statement is followed by several suggested answers or completions. Select the one that BEST answers the question or completes the statement. *PRINT THE LETTER OF THE CORRECT ANSWER IN THE SPACE AT THE RIGHT.*

Questions 1-4.

DIRECTIONS: Questions 1 through 4 consist of three sentences each. For each question, select the sentence which contains NO error in grammar or usage.

1. A. Be sure that everybody brings his notes to the conference.
    B. He looked like he meant to hit the boy.
    C. Mr. Jones is one of the clients who was chosen to represent the district.
    D. All are incorrect.

2. A. He is taller than I.
    B. I'll have nothing to do with these kind of people.
    C. The reason why he will not buy the house is because it is too expensive.
    D. All are incorrect.

3. A. Aren't I eligible for this apartment.
    B. Have you seen him anywheres?
    C. He should of come earlier.
    D. All are incorrect.

4. A. He graduated college in 2022.
    B. He hadn't but one more line to write.
    C. Who do you think is the author of this report?
    D. All are incorrect.

Questions 5-35.

DIRECTIONS: In each of the following questions, only one of the four sentences conforms to standards of correct usage. The other three contain errors in grammar, diction, or punctuation. Select the choice in each question which BEST conforms to standards of correct usage. Consider a choice correct if it contains none of the errors mentioned above, even though there may be other ways of expressing the same thought.

5. A. It is obvious that no one wants to be a kill-joy if they can help it.
    B. It is not always possible, and perhaps it never ispossible, to judge a person's character by just looking at him.
    C. When Yogi Berra of the New York Yankees hit an immortal grandslam home run, everybody in the huge stadium including Pittsburgh fans, rose to his feet.
    D. Every one of us students must pay tuition today.

2 (#2)

6. A. The physician told the young mother that if the baby is not able to digest its milk, it should be boiled.
    B. There is no doubt whatsoever that he felt deeply hurt because John Smith had betrayed the trust.
    C. Having partaken of a most delicious repast prepared by Tessie Breen, the hostess, the horses were driven home immediately thereafter.
    D. The attorney asked my wife and myself several questions.

6.____

7. A. Despite all denials, there is no doubt in my mind that
    B. At this time everyone must deprecate the demogogic attack made by one of our Senators on one of our most revered statesmen.
    C. In the first game of a crucial two-game series, Ted Williams, got two singles, both of them driving in a run.
    D. Our visitor brought good news to John and I.

7.____

8. A. If he would have told me, I should have been glad to help him in his dire financial emergency.
    B. Newspaper men have often asserted that diplomats or so-called official spokesmen sometimes employ equivocation in attempts to deceive.
    C. I think someones coming to collect money for the Red Cross.
    D. In a masterly summation, the young attorney expressed his belief that the facts clearly militate against this opinion.

8.____

9. A. We have seen most all the exhibits.
    B. Without in the least underestimating your advice, in my opinion the situation has grown immeasurably worse in the past few days.
    C. I wrote to the box office treasurer of the hit show that a pair of orchestra seats would be preferable.
    D. As the grim story of Pearl Harbor was broadcast on that fateful December 7, it was the general opinion that war was inevitable.

9.____

10. A. Without a moment's hesitation, Casey Stengel said that Larry Berra works harder than any player on the team.
    B. There is ample evidence to indicate that many animals can run faster than any human being.
    C. No one saw the accident but I.
    D. Example of courage is the heroic defense put up by the paratroopers against overwhelming odds.

10.____

11. A. If you prefer these kind, Mrs. Grey, we shall be more than willing to let you have them reasonably.
    B. If you like these here, Mrs. Grey, we shall be more than willing to let you have them reasonably.
    C. If you like these, Mrs. Grey, we shall be more than willing to let you have them.
    D. Who shall we appoint?

11.____

12. A. The number of errors are greater in speech than in writing.
    B. The doctor rather than the nurse was to blame for his being neglected.
    C. Because the demand for these books have been so great, we reduced the price.
    D. John Galsworthy, the English novelist, could not have survived a serious illness; had it not been for loving care.

12._____

13. A. Our activities this year have seldom ever been as interesting as they have been this month.
    B. Our activities this month have been more interesting, or at least as interesting as those of any month this year.
    C. Our activities this month has been more interesting than those of any other month this year.
    D. Neither Jean nor her sister was at home.

13._____

14. A. George B. Shaw's view of common morality, as well as his wit sparkling with a dash of perverse humor here and there, have led critics to term him "The Incurable Rebel."
    B. The President's program was not always received with the wholehearted endorsement of his own party, which is why the party faces difficulty in drawing up a platform for the coming election.
    C. The reason why they wanted to travel was because they had never been away from home.
    D. Facing a barrage of cameras, the visiting celebrity found it extremely difficult to express his opinions clearly.

14._____

15. A. When we calmed down, we all agreed that our anger had been kind of unnecessary and had not helped the situation.
    B. Without him going into all the details, he made us realize the horror of the accident.
    C. Like one girl, for example, who applied for two positions.
    D. Do not think that you have to be so talented as he is in order to play in the school orchestra.

15._____

16. A. He looked very peculiarly to me.
    B. He certainly looked at me peculiar.
    C. Due to the train's being late, we had to wait an hour.
    D. The reason for the poor attendance is that it is raining.

16._____

17. A. About one out of four own an automobile.
    B. The collapse of the old Mitchell Bridge was caused by defective construction in the central pier.
    C. Brooks Atkinson was well acquainted with the best literature, thus helping him to become an able critic.
    D. He has to stand still until the relief man comes up, thus giving him no chance to move about and keep warm.

17._____

18. A. He is sensitive to confusion and withdraws from people whom he feels are too noisy.
    B. Do you know whether the data is statistically correct?
    C. Neither the mayor or the aldermen are to blame.
    D. Of those who were graduated from high school, a goodly percentage went to college.

    18.____

19. A. Acting on orders, the offices were searched by a designated committee.
    B. The answer probably is nothing.
    C. I thought it to be all right to excuse them from class.
    D. I think that he is as successful a singer, if not more successful, than Mary.

    19.____

20. A. $360,000 is really very little to pay for such a wellbuilt house.
    B. The creatures looked like they had come from outer space.
    C. It was her, he knew!
    D. Nobody but me knows what to do.

    20.____

21. A. Mrs. Smith looked good in her new suit.
    B. New York may be compared with Chicago.
    C. I will not go to the meeting except you go with me.
    D. I agree with this editorial.

    21.____

22. A. My opinions are different from his.
    B. There will be less students in class now.
    C. Helen was real glad to find her watch.
    D. It had been pushed off of her dresser.

    22.____

23. A. Almost everyone, who has been to California, returns with glowing reports.
    B. George Washington, John Adams, and Thomas Jefferson, were our first presidents.
    C. Mr. Walters, whom we met at the bank yesterday, is the man, who gave me my first job.
    D. One should study his lessons as carefully as he can.

    23.____

24. A. We had such a good time yesterday.
    B. When the bell rang, the boys and girls went in the schoolhouse.
    C. John had the worst headache when he got up this morning.
    D. Today's assignment is somewhat longer than yesterday's.

    24.____

25. A. Neither the mayor nor the city clerk are willing to talk.
    B. Neither the mayor nor the city clerk is willing to talk.
    C. Neither the mayor or the city clerk are willing to talk.
    D Neither the mayor or the city clerk is willing to talk.

    25.____

26. A. Being that he is that kind of boy, cooperation cannot be expected.
    B. He interviewed people who he thought had something to say.
    C. Stop whomever enters the building regardless of rank or office held.
    D. Passing through the countryside, the scenery pleased us.

    26.____

27. A. The childrens' shoes were in their closet.
    B. The children's shoes were in their closet.
    C. The childs' shoes were in their closet.
    D. The childs' shoes were in his closet.

    27.____

28. A. An agreement was reached between the defendant, the plaintiff, the plaintiff's attorney and the insurance company as to the amount of the settlement.
    B. Everybody was asked to give their versions of the accident.
    C. The consensus of opinion was that the evidence was inconclusive.
    D. The witness stated that if he was rich, he wouldn't have had to loan the money.

    28.____

29. A. Before beginning the investigation, all the materials related to the case were carefully assembled.
    B. The reason for his inability to keep the appointment is because of his injury in the accident.
    C. This here evidence tends to support the claim of the defendant.
    D. We interviewed all the witnesses who, according to the driver, were still in town.

    29.____

30. A. Each claimant was allowed the full amount of their medical expenses.
    B. Either of the three witnesses is available.
    C. Every one of the witnesses was asked to tell his story.
    D. Neither of the witnesses are right.

    30.____

31. A. The commissioner, as well as his deputy and various bureau heads, were present.
    B. A new organization of employers and employees have been formed.
    C. One or the other of these men have been selected.
    D. The number of pages in the book is enough to discourage a reader.

    31.____

32. A. Between you and me, I think he is the better man.
    B. He was believed to be me.
    C. Is it us that you wish to see?
    D. The winners are him and her.

    32.____

33. A. Beside the statement to the police, the witness spoke to no one.
    B. He made no statement other than to the police and I.
    C. He made no statement to any one else, aside from the police.
    D. The witness spoke to no one but me.

    33.____

34. A. The claimant has no one to blame but himself.
    B. The boss sent us, he and I, to deliver the packages.
    C. The lights come from mine and not his car.
    D. There was room on the stairs for him and myself.

    34.____

6 (#2)

35. A. Admission to this clinic is limited to patients' inability to pay for medical care.
    B. Patients who can pay little or nothing for medical care are treated in this clinic.
    C. The patient's ability to pay for medical care is the determining factor in his admission to this clinic.
    D. This clinic is for the patient's that cannot afford to pay or that can pay a little for medical care.

35.____

KEY (CORRECT ANSWERS)

1.	A	11.	C	21.	A	31.	D
2.	A	12.	B	22.	A	32.	A
3.	D	13.	D	23.	D	33.	D
4.	C	14.	D	24.	D	34.	A
5.	D	15.	D	25.	B	35.	B
6.	D	16.	D	26.	B		
7.	B	17.	B	27.	B		
8.	B	18.	D	28.	C		
9.	D	19.	B	29.	D		
10.	B	20.	D	30.	C		

EXAMINATION SECTION
TEST 1

DIRECTIONS: Each question or incomplete statement is followed by several suggested answers or completions. Select the one that BEST answers the question or completes the statement. *PRINT THE LETTER OF THE CORRECT ANSWER IN THE SPACE AT THE RIGHT.*

1. Which of the following sentences is punctuated INCORRECTLY?
   A. Johnson said, "One tiny virus, Blanche, can multiply so fast that it will become 200 viruses in 25 minutes."
   B. With economic pressures hitting them from all sides, American farmers have become the weak link in the food chain.
   C. The degree to which this is true, of course, depends on the personalities of the people involved, the subject matter, and the atmosphere in general.
   D. "What loneliness, asked George Eliot, is more lonely than distrust?"

2. Which of the following sentences is punctuated INCORRECTLY?
   A. Based on past experiences, do you expect the plumber to show up late, not have the right parts, and overcharge you.
   B. When polled, however, the participants were most concerned that it be convenient.
   C. No one mentioned the flavor of the coffee, and no one seemed to care that china was used instead of plastic.
   D. As we said before, sometimes people view others as things; they don't see them as living, breathing beings like themselves.

3. Convention members travelled here from Kingston New York Pittsfield Massachusetts Bennington Vermont and Hartford Connecticut.
   How many commas should there be in the above sentence?
   A. 3 B. 4 C. 5 D. 6

4. Of the two speakers the one who spoke about human rights is more famous and more humble.
   How many commas should there be in the above sentence?
   A. 1 B. 2 C. 3 D. 4

5. Which sentence is punctuated INCORRECTLY?
   A. Five people voted no; two voted yes; one person abstained.
   B. Well, consider what has been said here today, but we won't make any promises.
   C. Anthropologists divide history into three major periods: the Stone Age, the Bronze Age, and the Iron Age.
   D. Therefore, we may create a stereotype about people who are unsuccessful; we may see them as lazy, unintelligent, or afraid of success.

6. Which sentence is punctuated INCORRECTLY?

   A. Studies have found that the unpredictability of customer behavior can lead to a great deal of stress, particularly if the behavior is unpleasant or if the employee has little control over it.
   B. If this degree of emotion and variation can occur in spectator sports, imagine the role that perceptions can play when there are <u>real</u> stakes involved.
   C. At other times, however hidden expectations may sabotage or severely damage an encounter without anyone knowing what happened.
   D. There are usually four issues to look for in a conflict: differences in values, goals, methods, and facts.

6.____

Questions 7-10.

DIRECTIONS: Questions 7 through 10 test your ability to distinguish between words that sound alike but are spelled differently and have different meanings. In the following groups of sentences, one of the underlined words is used incorrectly.

7. A. By <u>accepting</u> responsibility for their actions, managers promote trust.
    B. Dropping hints or making <u>illusions</u> to things that you would like changed sometimes leads to resentment.
    C. The entire unit <u>loses</u> respect for the manager and resents the reprimand.
    D. Many people are <u>averse</u> to confronting problems directly; they would rather avoid them.

7.____

8. A. What does this say about the <u>effect</u> our expectations have on those we supervise?
    B. In an effort to save time between 9 A.M. and 1 P.M., the staff members devised <u>their</u> own interpretation of what was to be done on these forms.
    C. The taskmaster's <u>principal</u> concern is for getting the work done; he or she is not concerned about the need or interests of employees.
    D. The advisor's main objective was increasing Angela's ability to invest her <u>capitol</u> wisely.

8.____

9. A. A typical problem is that people have to cope with the internal <u>censer</u> of their feelings.
    B. Sometimes, in their attempt to sound more learned, people speak in ways that are barely <u>comprehensible</u>.
    C. The <u>council</u> will meet next Friday to decide whether Abrams should continue as representative.
    D. His <u>descent</u> from grace was assured by that final word.

9.____

10. A. The doctor said that John's leg had to remain <u>stationary</u> or it would not heal properly.
    B. There is a city <u>ordinance</u> against parking too close to fire hydrants.
    C. Meyer's problem is that he is never <u>discrete</u> when talking about office politics.
    D. Mrs. Thatcher probably worked harder <u>than</u> any other British Prime Minister had ever worked.

10.____

3 (#1)

Questions 11-20.

DIRECTIONS: For each of the following groups of sentences in Questions 11 through 20, select the sentence which is the BEST example of English usage and grammar.

11. A. She is a woman who, at age sixty, is distinctly attractive and cares about how they look.
    B. It was a seemingly impossible search, and no one knew the problems better than she.
    C. On the surface, they are all sweetness and light, but his morbid character is under it.
    D. The minicopier, designed to appeal to those who do business on the run like architects in the field or business travelers, weigh about four pounds.

11.____

12. A. Neither the administrators nor the union representative regret the decision to settle the disagreement.
    B. The plans which are made earlier this year were no longer being considered.
    C. I would have rode with him if I had known he was leaving at five.
    D. I don't know who she said had it.

12.____

13. A. Writing at a desk, the memo was handed to her for immediate attention.
    B. Carla didn't water Carl's plants this week, which she never does.
    C. Not only are they good workers, with excellent writing and speaking skills, and they get to the crux of any problem we hand them.
    D. We've noticed that this enthusiasm for undertaking new projects sometimes interferes with his attention to detail.

13.____

14. A. It's obvious that Nick offends people by being unruly, inattentive, and having no patience.
    B. Marcia told Genie that she would have to leave soon.
    C. Here are the papers you need to complete your investigation.
    D. Julio was startled by you're comment.

14.____

15. A. The new manager has done good since receiving her promotion, but her secretary has helped her a great deal.
    B. One of the personnel managers approached John and tells him that the client arrived unexpectedly.
    C. If somebody can supply us with the correct figures, they should do so immediately.
    D. Like zealots, advocates seek power because they want to influence the policies and actions of an organization.

15.____

16. A. Between you and me, Chris probably won't finish this assignment in time. 16.____
    B. Rounding the corner, the snack bar appeared before us.
    C. Parker's radical reputation made to the Supreme Court his appointment impossible.
    D. By the time we arrived, Marion finishes briefing James and returns to Hank's office.

17. A. As we pointed out earlier, the critical determinant of the success of middle 17.____
       managers is their ability to communicate well with others.
    B. The lecturer stated there wasn't no reason for bad supervision.
    C. We are well aware whose at fault in this instance.
    D. When planning important changes, it's often wise to seek the participation of others because employees often have much valuable ideas to offer.

18. A. Joan had ought to throw out those old things that were damaged when the 18.____
       roof leaked.
    B. I spose he'll let us know what he's decided when he finally comes to a decision.
    C. Carmen was walking to work when she suddenly realized that she had left her lunch on the table as she passed the market.
    D. Are these enough plants for your new office?

19. A. First move the lever forward, and then they should lift the ribbon casing 19.____
       before trying to take it out.
    B. Michael finished quickest than any other person in the office.
    C. There is a special meeting for we committee members today at 4 p.m.
    D. My husband is worried about our having to work overtime next week.

20. A. Another source of conflicts are individuals who possess very poor 20.____
       interpersonal skills.
    B. It is difficult for us to work with him on projects because these kinds of people are not interested in team building.
    C. Each of the departments was represented at the meeting.
    D. Poor boy, he never should of past that truck on the right.

Questions 21-28.

DIRECTIONS: In Questions 21 through 28, there may be a problem with English grammar or usage. If a problem does exist, select the letter that indicates the most effective change. If no problem exists, select Choice A.

21. He rushed her to the hospital and stayed with her, even though this took quite a 21.____
    bit of his time, he didn't charge her anything.
       A. No changes are necessary.
       B. Change even though to although
       C. Change the first comma to a period and capitalize even
       D. Change rushed to had rushed

5 (#1)

22. Waiting that appears unfairly feels longer than waiting that seems justified. 22.____
    A. No changes are necessary.
    B. Change unfairly to unfair
    C. Change appears to seems
    D. Change longer to longest

23. May be you and the person who argued with you will be able to reach an agreement. 23.____
    A. No changes are necessary
    B. Change will be to were
    C. Change argued with to had an argument with
    D. Change May be to Maybe

24. Any one of them could of taken the file while you were having coffee. 24.____
    A. No changes are necessary
    B. Change any one to anyone
    C. Change of to have
    D. Change were having to were out having

25. While people get jobs or move from poverty level to better paying employment, they stop receiving benefits and start paying taxes. 25.____
    A. No changes are necessary
    B. Change While to As
    C. Change stop to will stop
    D. Change get to obtain

26. Maribeth's phone rang while talking to George about the possibility of their meeting Tom at three this afternoon. 26.____
    A. No changes are necessary
    B. Change their to her
    C. Move to George so that it follows Tom
    D. Change talking to she was talking

27. According to their father, Lisa is smarter than Chris, but Emily is the smartest of the three sisters. 27.____
    A. No changes are necessary
    B. Change their to her
    C. Change is to was
    D. Make two sentences, changing the second comma to a period and omitting but

28. Yesterday, Mark and he claim that Carl took Carol's ideas and used them inappropriately. 28.____
    A. No changes are necessary
    B. Change claim to claimed
    C. Change inappropriately to inappropriate
    D. Change Carol's to Carols'

Questions 29-34.

DIRECTIONS: For each group of sentences in Questions 29 through 34, select the choice that represents the BEST editing of the problem sentence.

29. The managers expected employees to be at their desks at all times, but they would always be late or leave unannounced.
    A. The managers wanted employees to always be at their desks, but they would always be late or leave unannounced.
    B. Although the managers expected employees to be at their desks no matter what came up, they would always be late and leave without telling anyone.
    C. Although the managers expected employees to be at their desks at all times, the managers would always be late or leave without telling anyone.
    D. The managers expected the employee to never leave their desks, but they would always be late or leave without telling anyone.

29.____

30. The one who is department manager he will call you to discuss the problem tomorrow morning at 10 A.M.
    A. The one who is department manager will call you tomorrow morning at ten to discuss the problem.
    B. The department manager will call you to discuss the problem tomorrow at 10 A.M.
    C. Tomorrow morning at 10 A.M., the department manager will call you to discuss the problem.
    D. Tomorrow morning the department manager will call you to discuss the problem.

30.____

31. A conference on child care in the workplace the $200 cost of which to attend may be prohibitive to childcare workers who earn less than that weekly.
    A. A conference on child care in the workplace that costs $200 may be too expensive for childcare workers who earn less than that each week.
    B. A conference on child care in the workplace, the cost of which to attend is $200, may be prohibitive to childcare workers who earn less than that weekly.
    C. A conference on child care in the workplace who costs $200 may be too expensive for childcare workers who earn less than that a week.
    D. A conference on child care in the workplace which costs $200 may be too expensive to childcare workers who earn less than that on a weekly basis.

31.____

32. In accordance with estimates recently made, there are 40,000 to 50,000 nuclear weapons in our world today.
    A. Because of estimates recently, there are 40,000 to 50,000 nuclear weapons in the world today.
    B. In accordance with estimates made recently, there are 40,000 to 50,000 nuclear weapons in the world today.

32.____

C. According to estimates made recently, there are 40,000 to 50,000 weapons in the world today.
D. According to recent estimates, there are 40,000 to 50,000 nuclear weapons in the world today.

33. Motivation is important in problem solving, but they say that excessive motivation can inhibit the creative process.
    A. Motivation is important in problem solving, but, as they say, too much of it can inhibit the creative process.
    B. Motivation is important in problem solving and excessive motivation will inhibit the creative process.
    C. Motivation is important in problem solving, but excessive motivation can inhibit the creative process.
    D. Motivation is important in problem solving because excessive motivation can inhibit the creative process.

33.____

34. In selecting the best option calls for consulting with all the people that are involved in it.
    A. In selecting the best option consulting with all people concerned with it.
    B. Calling for the best option, we consulted all the affected people.
    C. We called all the people involved to select the best option.
    D. To be sure of selecting the best option, one should consult all the people involved.

34.____

35. There are a number of problems with the following letter. From the options below, select the version that is MOST in accordance with standard business style, tone, and form.

35.____

Dear Sir:

    We are so sorry that we have had to backorder your order for 15,000 widgets and 2,300 whatzits for such a long time. We have been having incredibly bad luck lately. When your order first came in no one could get to it because my secretary was out with the flu and her replacement didn't know what she was doing, then there was the dock strike in Cucamonga which held things up for awhile, and then it just somehow got lost. We think it may have fallen behind the radiator.
    We are happy to say that all these problems have been taken care of, we are caught up on supplies, and we should have the stuff to you soon, in the near future—about two weeks. You may not believe us after everything you've been through with us, but it's true.
    We'll let you know as soon as we have a secure date for delivery. Thank you so much for continuing to do business with us after all the problems this probably has caused you.

Yours very sincerely,
Rob Barker

A. Dear Sir:

    We are so sorry that we have had to backorder your order for 15,000 widgets and 2,300 whatzits. We have been having problems with staff lately and the dock strike hasn't helped anything.
    We are happy to say that all these problems have been taken care of. I've told my secretary to get right on it, and we should have the stuff to you soon. Thank you so much for continuing to do business with us after all the problems this must have caused you.
    We'll let you know as soon as we have a secure date for delivery.

Sincerely,
Rob Barker

B. Dear Sir:

    We regret that we haven't been able to fill your order for 15,000 widgets and 2,300 whatzits in a timely fashion.
    We'll let you know as soon as we have a secure date for delivery.

Sincerely,
Rob Barker

C. Dear Sir:

    We are so very sorry that we haven't been able to fill your order for 15,000 widgets and 2,300 whatzits. We have been having incredibly bad luck lately, but things are much better now.
    Thank you so much for bearing with us through all of this. We'll let you know as soon as we have a secure date for delivery.

Sincerely,
Rob Barker

D. Dear Sir:

    We are very sorry that we haven't been able to fill your order for 15,000 widgets and 2,300 whatzits. Due to unforeseen difficulties, we have had to back-order your request. At this time, supplies have caught up to demand, and we foresee a delivery date within the next two weeks.
    We'll let you know as soon as we have a secure date for delivery. Thank you for your patience.

Sincerely,
Rob Barker

KEY (CORRECT ANSWERS)

1.	D	11.	B	21.	C	31.	A
2.	A	12.	D	22.	B	32.	D
3.	B	13.	D	23.	D	33.	C
4.	A	14.	C	24.	C	34.	D
5.	B	15.	D	25.	B	35.	D
6.	C	16.	A	26.	D		
7.	B	17.	A	27.	A		
8.	D	18.	D	28.	B		
9.	A	19.	D	29.	C		
10.	C	20.	C	30.	B		

EXAMINATION SECTION
TEST 1

DIRECTIONS: Each question or incomplete statement is followed by several suggested answers or completions. Select the one that BEST answers the question or completes the statement. *PRINT THE LETTER OF THE CORRECT ANSWER IN THE SPACE AT THE RIGHT.*

1. Our number system has a base of
   A. 2   B. 5   C. 10   D. 60

   1._____

2. To find the average weight of the football team,
   A. add and divide
   B. multiply
   C. add
   D. divide the weight of each player

   2._____

3. The thermometer used to measure the temperature of a school is called
   A. Centigrade
   B. Fahrenheit
   C. fever thermometer
   D. gauge

   3._____

4. The value of a fraction is changed when the same number is _____ to both numerator and denominator.
   A. added
   B. divided
   C. multiplied
   D. reduced to both terms of the fraction

   4._____

5. Stores buy their merchandise from firms called
   A. commissioners
   B. retail firms
   C. factories
   D. wholesale firms

   5._____

6. The amount of money you borrow is called the
   A. amount
   B. discount
   C. principal
   D. bank discount

   6._____

7. An angle of 75° is called a(n) _____ angle.
   A. acute   B. obtuse   C. straight   D. right

   7._____

8. The rate of interest could be found by the formula
   A. $I = Prt$ B. $r = i/pt$ C. $r = Pt$ D. $I = P/Rt$

   8._____

9. If three sides of one triangle are equal to the three sides of the other, the triangles are
   A. equilateral
   B. right triangles
   C. scalene
   D. congruent

   9._____

10. A rectangular solid could be called a(n)
    A. plane
    B. irregular figure
    C. polygon
    D. prism

    10._____

11. A written promise to repay the face of a loan is a
    A. refund
    B. promissory note
    C. dividend
    D. deposit

    11._____

12. The ² written above the s in the formula As² means
    A. 2s
    B. s × s
    C. s + s
    D. s/2

    12._____

13. Selling price includes cost plus profit plus
    A. expenses
    B. profit
    C. loss
    D. net price

    13._____

14. When numbers are used to express how many or how much of units of measure, they are called
    A. digits
    B. denominate numbers
    C. integers
    D. whole numbers

    14._____

15. The square of a number is that number multiplied by
    A. two
    B. twice the number
    C. four
    D. itself

    15._____

16. When the merchant permits the customer to make a down payment and make regular payments on an article, this form of payment is called
    A. dues
    B. rent
    C. installment buying
    D. utility payments

    16._____

17. Circles that have a common center and different radii are _____ circles.
    A. equal
    B. center
    C. congruent
    D. concentric

    17._____

18. The United States standard of measure of length is the
    A. base 10
    B. meter
    C. English system
    D. metric system

    18._____

19. If you put money to work for you, the income you receive is called
    A. income taxes
    B. interest
    C. bank discount
    D. sales tax

    19._____

20. A fraction whose numerator is a fraction and denominator is an integer is a _____ fraction.
    A. common
    B. decimal
    C. improper
    D. complex

    20._____

KEY (CORRECT ANSWERS)

1.	C	11.	B
2.	A	12.	B
3.	B	13.	A
4.	A	14.	B
5.	D	15.	D
6.	C	16.	C
7.	A	17.	D
8.	B	18.	C
9.	D	19.	B
10.	D	20.	D

SOLUTIONS TO PROBLEMS

1. 10 is the base of our number system. Ex: 456 = (4)(10²) + (5)(10) + 6.

2. To find the average weight, add and divide.

3. Fahrenheit degrees would be used for schools.

4. A fraction will change when the same number is added to both numerator and denominator. Ex: Add 5 to both parts of 2/3 to get /8, and 7/8 ≠ 2/3.

5. Stores buy merchandise from wholesale firms.

6. Principal = amount of money borrowed.

7. 75° is an acute angle since it is less than 90°.

8. R = I/(PT) shows rate in terms of interest, principal, and time.

9. If 3 sides of one triangle match 3 sides of a second triangle, they are congruent (SSS).

10. A rectangular solid is a special kind of prism.

11. Promissory note = written promise to repay a loan.

12. s² = s × s

13. Selling price includes cost, profit, and expenses.

14. Denominate numbers express units of measure. Ex: 8 gallons.

15. Square of any number = that number times itself. Ex: 4² = 4 × 4 = 16.

16. Installment buying = down payment + regular payments. Ex: $1000 down payment + $300 payment per month for 2 years.

17. Concentric circles have a common center but different radii. Diagram appears as:

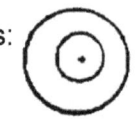

18. The English system is the U.S. standard measure of length. This includes inches, feet, yards, miles, etc.

19. Interest = income received when money is put to work (invested).

20. A complex fraction would contain a fraction within its numerator, denominator, or both.

Ex 1: $\dfrac{\frac{1}{2}}{\frac{1}{3}} = \dfrac{1}{2} \cdot \dfrac{3}{1} = \dfrac{3}{2}$

Ex 2: $\dfrac{1/2}{3} = \dfrac{1}{2} \cdot \dfrac{1}{3} = \dfrac{1}{6}$

Ex 3: $\dfrac{\frac{1}{2}}{3} = \dfrac{1}{1} \cdot \dfrac{3}{2} = \dfrac{3}{2}$

TEST 2

DIRECTIONS: Each question or incomplete statement is followed by several suggested answers or completions. Select the one that BEST answers the question or completes the statement. *PRINT THE LETTER OF THE CORRECT ANSWER IN THE SPACE AT THE RIGHT.*

1. Sally is going to Chicago for a visit. The bus fare is $27.85 one way or a round-trip ticket would be $51.56.
   How much can Sally save by buying a round-trip ticket rather than two one-way tickets?
   A. $4.20
   B. $2.07
   C. $4.14
   D. None of the above

   1.____

2. The Webster Junior High School collected $226.45 for Junior Red Cross and $420.55 for the Community Chest. There were 850 students in the school.
   To the NEAREST cent, what was the average contribution?
   A. $.76
   B. $.50
   C. $1.00
   D. None of the above

   2.____

3. Jack borrowed $57.50 from his father and agreed to pay it in twelve monthly payments of $5.00 each.
   How much interest did he pay?
   A. $2.50
   B. $3.50
   C. $7.50
   D. None of the above

   3.____

4. Joe's mother bought a roast weighing 6 ¾ lbs. at 89¢ a pound.
   How much change did she receive from a $10.00 bill?
   A. $3.99
   B. $5.01
   C. $6.01
   D. None of the above

   4.____

5. The Athletic Department paid $45 total tax on 1,000 tickets.
   How much tax was this per ticket?
   A. $.22
   B. $.45
   C. 4.5 cents
   D. None of the above

   5.____

6. Mary bought 4½ yards of lace. She used 1⅔ yards of it on a blouse.
   _____ yards of lace were left.
   A. 3 ⅙
   B. 3 ½
   C. 2 ⅚
   D. None of the above

   6.____

7. The girls are going to make aprons for Junior Red Cross. The pattern calls for ¾ yard of material for one apron.
   They will need _____ yards for 25 aprons.
   A. 33 ⅓
   B. 18 ¾
   C. 20
   D. None of the above

   7.____

2 (#2)

8. Which city on a world map of standard time zones would be NEAR the 75°W? 8.____
   A. Greenwich B. Sydney
   C. Calcutta D. None of the above

9. John's father made a down payment on a car and has $1,320 left to pay. 9.____
   He pays $55 each month.
   It will take him _____ months to finish the car payments.
   A. 42 B. 24
   C. 18 D. None of the above

10. Pete bought a board 12 ft. 8 in. long from which he wants to make three shelves. 10.____
    Two of the shelves are 2 ft. 8 in. long, and the third shelf is 1 ft. 6 in. long.
    How long will the piece be that is left over?
    A. 5 ft. 8 in. B. 5 ft. 10 in.
    C. 6 ft. 10 in. D. None of the above

11. A factory worker received an increase of 15% in his hourly wages. His former 11.____
    wages were $1.80 per hour.
    How much a week did his wages INCREASE in a forty-hour week?
    A. $21.17 B. $8.00
    C. $10.80 D. None of the above

12. Find the installment price of a washing machine if the down payment is 12.____
    $39.90, the monthly payments are $14.13 for twelve months, and the interest
    charge is $9.86.
    A. $179.52 B. $219.42
    C. $169.56 D. None of the above

13. How many hundreds in 18762? 13.____
    A. 7 B. 87
    C. 187 D. None of the above

14. The football team won 16 games and lost 4 games. 14.____
    What percent of the games played did they win?
    A. 75% B. 80%
    C. 40% D. None of the above

15. The bakery boxed doughnuts one half dozen to a box. 15.____
    They will have _____ full boxes if they fry 500 doughnuts.
    A. 41 B. 83
    C. 82 D. None of the above

16. Jane's parents burn fuel oil. They have used 180 gallons. The gauge indicates 16.____
    the tank is 5/8 full.
    The tank holds _____ gallons.
    A. 255 B. 480
    C. 600 D. None of the above

3 (#2)

17. _____ tiles, each a 9" square, could be laid in one width of a recreation room that is 25 feet long and 16½ feet wide.
    A. 22
    B. 149
    C. 51
    D. None of the above

17._____

18. The outside diameter of a wheel on Bob's bicycle is 28 inches. The outside diameter of a wheel on his little brother's bicycle is 21 inches. After traveling a mile, the little brother's wheel will make _____ revolutions more.
    A. 1080
    B. 269.5
    C. 240
    D. None of the above

18._____

19. Bill gets 17 ¾ miles per gallon.
    At this rate, he should get _____ miles if he buys 5.6 gallons of gasoline.
    A. 317
    B. 99.4
    C. 85
    D. None of the above

19._____

20. The scale drawing of a house is 1 in. = 12 ft.
    If a room is 33 feet long, a _____ inch line should be used on the blueprint to represent that distance.
    A. 2 ¾
    B. 3.3
    C. 2.1`
    D. None of the above

20._____

21. A 2-inch gear makes 75 revolutions per minute.
    A 3-inch fear makes _____ rpm at the same rate of speed.
    A. 12 ½
    B. 112 ½
    C. 50
    D. None of the above

21._____

22. What is the selling price of a radio that cost the dealer $36 and the margin is 40% of the selling price?
    A. $60
    B. $45
    C. $50.40
    None of the above

22._____

23. Mr. Jacks used 35 kwh.
    If the charge is 8¢ a kwh for the first 20 kwh and 5¢ for the remainder, what was the TOTAL charge?
    A. $2.35
    B. $3.35
    C. $4.55
    D. None of the above

23._____

24. Druggists use a unit of measurement of weight called the grain. There are *approximately* 437.5 grains in one ounce.
    There are APPROXIMATELY _____ grains in a pound.
    A. 7000
    B. 5252
    C. 73,400
    D. None of the above

24._____

25. A gasoline tank is 16 ft. high and has a diameter of 14 ft.
    The tank will hold _____ cubic feet of gasoline (use 22/7 for pi) to the NEAREST 10 cu. ft.
    A. 704
    B. 784
    C. 2460
    D. None of the above

25._____

KEY (CORRECT ANSWERS)

1.	C	11.	C
2.	A	12.	B
3.	A	13.	C
4.	A	14.	B
5.	C	15.	B
6.	C	16.	B
7.	B	17.	A
8.	D	18.	C
9.	B	19.	B
10.	B	20.	A

21. C
22. A
23. A
24. A
25. C

SOLUTIONS TO PROBLEMS

1. Savings = ($27.85)(2) - $51.56 = $4.14

2. Average contribution = ($226.45 + $420.55) ÷ 850 = $647 ÷ 850 ≈ $.76

3. Interest = (12)($5.00) - $57.50 = $2.50

4. $10.00 − (6.75)(.89) = $3.99 change

5. $45 ÷ 1000 = .045 = 4.5 cents tax per ticket

6. 4 1/2 − 1 2/3 = 4 3/6 − 1 4/6 − 1 = 2 5.6 yds, left

7. (3/4)(25) = 18 3/4 yds. needed

8. Refer to world map. None is correct.

9. $1320 ÷ 55 = 24 months

10. 12'8" − 2'8" − 2'8" − 1'6" = 152" − 32" − 32" − 18" = 70" = 5'10"

11. Increase = ($1.80)(.15)(40) = $10.80 per week

12. $39.90 + ($14.13)(12) + $9.96 = $219.42 installment price

13. 18,762 ÷ 100 = 187 with remainder of 62. So, there are 187 hundreds in 18,762.

14. Percent won = 16/20 = 80%

15. 500 ÷ 6 = 83 1/3, which means 83 full boxes + 1/3 of a box

16. 180 gallons represents 3/8 of the entire tank. Thus, the tank's capacity = 180 ÷ 3/8 = 480 gallons

17. 25' = 300" and 16 1/2' = 198". Now, 300 ÷ 9 = 33 1.3 and 198 ÷ 9 = 22. Then the number of tiles that could fit in 1 width = 22. (The actual number of tiles that could fit in the entire room = (22)(33) = 726)

18. 1 revolution of Bob's bicycle = 2π = $(2 \times \frac{22}{7} \times 14)$ = 88"

    1 revolution of his brother's bicycle = 2π = $(2 \times \frac{22}{7} \times 10.5)$ = 66"

19. $(17\frac{3}{4})(5.6) = (17.75)(5.6) = 99.4$ miles

20. $33 \div 12 = 2$ 3/4-inch line needed.

21. Let x = rpm. $2/3 = x/75$. Solving, x = 50.
    Note: Size of gear is inversely related to rpm.

22. Let x = selling price. Then, $36 = .60x$. Solving, x = $60.

23. Total charge = $(.08)(20) + (.05)(15) = \$2.35$

24. $(437.5)(16) = 7000$ grains in a pound (approx.)

25. Volume = $(\pi)(7^2)(16) \approx 2460$ cu. ft.

EXAMINATION SECTION
TEST 1

DIRECTIONS: Each question or incomplete statement is followed by several suggested answers or completions. Select the one that BEST answers the question or completes the statement. *PRINT THE LETTER OF THE CORRECT ANSWER IN THE SPACE AT THE RIGHT.*

1. 6.030 - 5.008 =

   A. 1.922   B. 1.092   C. .922   D. 1.022

2. $\dfrac{3}{8} \times \dfrac{2}{3} =$

   A. $1\dfrac{1}{4}$ B. $\dfrac{5}{8}$ C. $\dfrac{1}{3}$ D. $\dfrac{1}{4}$

3. $2 \times 3\dfrac{3}{4} =$

   A. $7\dfrac{3}{4}$ B. $6\dfrac{3}{4}$ C. $7\dfrac{1}{2}$ D. $6\dfrac{1}{2}$

4. $\dfrac{1}{6} + \dfrac{1}{4} + \dfrac{1}{2} =$

   A. $\dfrac{11}{12}$ B. $\dfrac{7}{6}$ C. $\dfrac{3}{12}$ D. 1

5. If 367 + 26 = 373 + n, n =

   A. 0   B. 2   C. 6   D. 20

6. $\dfrac{5}{8} \div 4 =$

   A. $2\dfrac{1}{2}$ B. $1\dfrac{1}{8}$ C. $\dfrac{5}{32}$ D. $\dfrac{1}{8}$

7. 3 hours 5 minutes
   -2 hours 55 minutes

   A. 1 hr. 10 min.   B. 1 hr. 5 min.
   C. 50 min.   D. 10 min.

1.____
2.____
3.____
4.____
5.____
6.____
7.____

121

8. If $\frac{3}{8} = \frac{n}{24}$, n =

   A. 16   B. 9   C. 5   D. 3

9. If 336 ÷ 8 = 40 + n, n =

   A. 4 1/2   B. 2   C. 3/4   D. 0

10. What is the sum of 2 feet 2 inches and 1 foot 6 inches?

    A. 1 yd. 2'8"
    C. 1 yd. 8"
    B. 1 yd. 1'8"
    D. 3 yd. 8"

11. 30% of 30 =

    A. 9.0   B. 0.9   C. 90.0   D. 60.0

12. $\frac{1}{6} - \frac{1}{7} =$

    A. 1/42
    C. 1
    B. 1/13
    D. none of the above

13. If 5/8 = 45/n, n =

    A. 40   B. 48   C. 64   D. 72

14. What is 1 yard 4 inches divided by 2?

    A. 10"   B. 1'2"   C. 1'8"   D. 1'10"

15. 1 foot 6 inches is what percent of one yard?

    A. 40   B. 50   C. 60   D. 200

16. If the scale on a road map is *twelve miles to one inch,* a road 112 miles long would be represented by a line

    A. 12"   B. 11 1/5"   C. 10"   D. 9 1/4"

17. During a sale a $25 toaster was reduced 15%. What was the sale price?

    A. $24.50   B. $21.25   C. $22.50   D. $20.00

18. 89 is 89% of

    A. 189   B. 100   C. 89   D. 1

19. If a man has a step which averages 32 inches, how many steps would he take to cover 16 feet?

    A. 2   B. 5   C. 6   D. 20

20. Sum is to difference as product is to

    A. subtrahend
    C. divisor
    B. multiplicand
    D. quotient

3 (#1)

21. Which of the following has the GREATEST value?   21._____

    A. 3% of 600   B. 2% of 800   C. 4% of 400   D. 5% of 200

22. 8.3% is equivalent to   22._____

    A. .0083   B. .083   C. .83   D. 8.3

23. What number must be put in the $\triangle$'s to make $(3x\triangle) - (2+\triangle)$ equal 14?   23._____

    A. 8   B. 7   C. 6   D. 3

24. The number nine thousand twenty and sixteen thousandths can be written   24._____

    A. 9020.160   B. 9020.016   C. 9020.0016   D. 920.016

25. If a plane that uses 40 gallons of gasoline per hour is to take a 6-hour trip and carry 10% extra gasoline for safety, how many gallons of gasoline should be put in the plane?   25._____

    A. 244   B. 246   C. 240.6   D. 264

26. If $103 \times 200 = 600 + n$, $n =$ 26._____

    A. (100x200)   B. (103x100)   C. (3x600)   D. (10x200)

27. What number must be put in the n to make $6 \times \dfrac{7}{\square}$ equal 14?   27._____

    A. 7   B. 6   C. 3   D. 2

Questions 28-30.

DIRECTIONS: Questions 28 through 30 are to be answered on the basis of the following graph.

1999 PROJECTIONS OF REGULAR SESSION COLLEGE ENROLLMENT FOR THE 2000'S

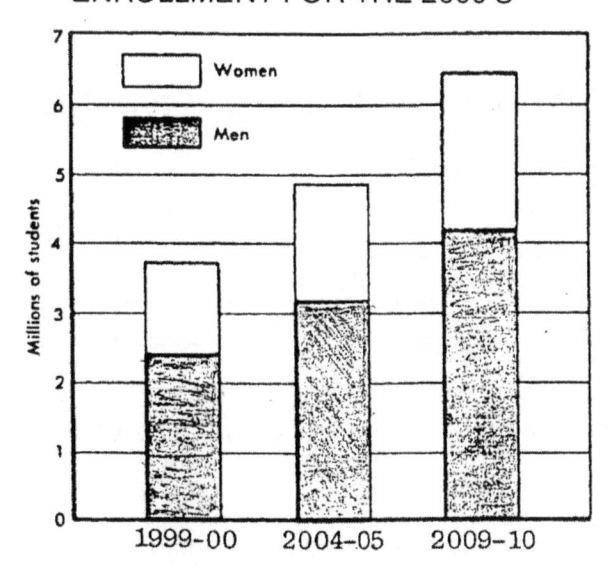

28. The increase in the number of men students from 2004-05 to 2009-2010 is expected to be about

   A. 10,000,000 B. 5,000,000
   C. 1,000,000   D. 500,000

29. Which of the following would be the BEST estimate of the number of men that will be in college in 2007-08?

   A. 5,600,000 B. 5,000,000
   C. 4,100,000 D. 3,700,000

30. It is predicted that the number of college women in 2009-10 will be APPROXIMATELY

   A. 220,000   B. 640,000   C. 2,200,000   D. 6,400,000

31. Which of the following is of greatest value?

   A. 11/16   B. .812   C. 5/8   D. .789

32. If a particular type of mail advertisement brings 20% response, how many copies of the advertisement should be sent to get 500 responses?

   A. 500   B. 2500   C. 1000   D. 5000

33. In one town tomatoes are selling at 3 pounds for 72 cents. At this rate, how much would you pay for 3 1/2 pounds?

   A. $1.32   B. $1.08   C. $0.96   D. $0.84

34. If a ridge in a piece of machinery is to have a length of 27/100 inch plus or minus 8/1000 inch, an inspector would accept a ridge with a length of

   A. 20/100"   B. 29/100"   C. 263/1000"   D. 301/1000"

Questions 35-37.

DIRECTIONS: Questions 35 through 37 are to be answered on the basis of the following table.

SHOOTING RECORD OF THE MEMBERS OF A BASKETBALL TEAM

Player	Shots Attempted	Shots Made
Jones	27	11
Smith	5	0
Allen	18	8
Lyons	11	5
Olson	14	2

35. The five players as a team made approximately what percent of their shots?

   A. 20   B. 25   C. 30   D. 35

36. Which player has the highest ratio of number of shots made to number of shots attempted?

   A. Lyons   B. Allen   C. Jones   D. Olson

37. If Allen had taken as many shots as Jones and maintained his shooting rate, how many shots would he have made?

   A. 13   B. 12   C. 11   D. 10

38. If each ring of a telephone bell is 1.1 seconds long with .6 second between rings, the time from the beginning of the first ring to the end of the sixth ring would be _____ sec.

   A. 6.6   B. 9.6   C. 13.2   D. 10.2

39. $\sqrt{.04} =$

   A. .2   B. .02   C. .002   D. 2.00

40. $3^2 =$

   A. $\sqrt{81}$ B. 2^3 C. $\sqrt{3}$ D. $\sqrt[3]{2}$

Questions 41-43.

DIRECTIONS: Questions 41 through 43 are to be answered on the basis of the following values.

   ⌂ represents the value of one chair
   ↑ represents the value of one umbrella
   ✧ represents the value of one belt

The value of a chair ⌂ is 12 times the value of an umbrella ↑, and the value of an umbrella is five times the value of a belt ✧.

   ⌂ = 12 ↑   ↑ = 5 ✧

41. 2 ↑ - 3 ✧ =

   A. ↑ + ✧   B. ↑ + 2 ✧   C. 6 ✧   D. 2 ✧

42. The difference between 2 ⌂ + 3 ✧ and ⌂ + ↑ + 4 ✧ is

   A. ⌂ + 11 ↑ + ✧   B. ⌂ - ✧   C. 10 ↑ + 4 ✧   D. 9 ✧

43. 15 ✧ =

   A. 1/3 ↑   B. 4 ↑   C. 1/4 ⌂   D. ⌂

44. The number 40, base ten, would be written 1111 in base

   A. three   B. two   C. four   D. twelve

45. If we write all numbers in base eight notation, $24_{eight} + 15_{eight} + 12_{eight} =$

   A. 51_{eight} B. 52_{eight} C. 54_{eight} D. 53_{eight}

KEY (CORRECT ANSWERS)

1. D	11. A	21. A	31. B	41. B
2. D	12. A	22. B	32. B	42. C
3. C	13. D	23. A	33. D	43. C
4. A	14. C	24. B	34. C	44. A
5. D	15. B	25. D	35. D	45. A
6. C	16. D	26. A	36. A	
7. D	17. B	27. C	37. B	
8. B	18. B	28. C	38. B	
9. B	19. C	29. D	39. A	
10. C	20. D	30. C	40. A	

SOLUTIONS TO PROBLEMS

1. $6.030 - 5.008 = 1.022$

2. $\dfrac{3}{8} \times \dfrac{2}{3} = \dfrac{6}{24} = \dfrac{1}{4}$

3. $2 \times 3\dfrac{3}{4} = \dfrac{2}{1} \times \dfrac{15}{4} = \dfrac{30}{4} = 7\dfrac{1}{2}$

4. $\dfrac{1}{6} + \dfrac{1}{4} + \dfrac{1}{2} = \dfrac{2}{12} + \dfrac{3}{12} + \dfrac{6}{12} = \dfrac{11}{12}$

5. $367 + 26 = 373 + n$, $n = 367 + 26 - 373 = 20$

6. $\dfrac{5}{8} \div 4 = \dfrac{5}{8} \times \dfrac{1}{4} = \dfrac{5}{32}$

7. 3 hrs. 5 min. - 2 hrs. 55 min. = 2 hrs. 65 min. - 2 hrs. 55 min. = 10 min.

8. $\dfrac{3}{8} = \dfrac{n}{24}$, $8n = 72$, $n = 9$

9. $336 \div 8 = 40 + n$, $42 = 40 + n$, $n = 2$

10. 2 ft. 2 in. + 1 ft. 6 in. = 3 ft. 8 in. = 1 yd. 8 in.

11. 30% of 30 = .30 × 30 = 9

12. $\dfrac{1}{6} - \dfrac{1}{7} = \dfrac{7}{42} - \dfrac{6}{42} = \dfrac{1}{42}$

13. $\dfrac{5}{8} = \dfrac{45}{n}$, $5n = 360$, $n = 72$

14. (1 yd. 4 in.) ÷ 2 = 40 in. ÷ 2 = 20 in. = 1 ft. 8 in.

15. 1 ft. 6 in. ÷ 1 yd. = 18 in. ÷ 36 in. = 1/2 = 50%

16. 112 ÷ 12 = 9 1/3 in.

17. Sale price = ($25)(.85) = $21.25

18. 89 = 89% of x, x = 89 ÷ .89 = 100

19. 16 ft. ÷ 32 in. = 192 in. ÷ 32 in. = 6 steps

20. Sum : Difference = Product : Quotient

21. 3% of 600 = 18, 2% of 800 = 16, 4% of 400 = 16,
    5% of 200 = 10. 3% of 600 is highest.

22. 8.3% = .083

23. 3 x △ - (2+ △) = 2 x △ - 2 = 14. △ = (14+2)/2 = 8

24. Nine thousand twenty and sixteen thousandths = 9020.016

25. (40)(6) + (.10)(40)(6) = 264 gallons

26. 103 x 200 = 600 + n; 20,600 = 600 + n; n = 20,000 = 100 x 200

27. $6 \times \frac{7}{\square} = 14$, $\frac{7}{\square} = \frac{14}{6}$, $14 \times \square = 42$, $\square = 3$

28. Increase ≈ 4.25 million - 3.25 million = 1,000,000

29. Roughly halfway between 3.25 million and 4.25 million ≈ 3,700,000

30. 6.5 million - 4.25 million = 2.25 million ≈ 2,200,000

31. 11/16 = .6875 and 5/8 = .625, so selection B (.812) has the largest value of the given selections.

32. Let x = number of copies sent. Then 500 = .20x, x = 2500

33. .72 ÷ 3 = .24 per pound. Then, (.24)(3 1/2) = .84

34. $\frac{27}{100} \pm \frac{8}{1000} = \frac{262}{1000}$ to $\frac{278}{1000}$. So, $\frac{263}{1000}$ is acceptable.

35. (11+0+8+5+2)/(27+5+18+11+14) = 26/75 ≈ 35%

36. Lyons: 5/11 = 45.$\overline{45}$%; Allen: 8/18 = 44.$\overline{4}$%; Jones: 11/27 = 40.$\overline{740}$%;

    Olson: 2/14 ≈ 14.3%. Lyons has the highest ratio.

37. Allen's ratio = 44.$\overline{4}$%. Then, (.$\overline{4}$)(27) = 12 shots made.

38. Total time = (6)(1.1) + (5)(.6) = 9.6 sec.

9 (#1)

39. $\sqrt{.04} = .2$

40. $3^2 = (3)(3) = 9 = \sqrt{81}$

41. $2\text{T} - 3\text{H} - = 10\text{H} - 3\text{H} = 7\text{H} = \text{T} + 2\text{H}$

42. $(2\text{h} + 3\text{H}) - (\text{h} + \text{T} + 4\text{H}) = \text{h} - \text{T} - \text{H} = 54\text{H} = 10\text{T} + 4\text{H}$

43. $15\text{H} = 3\text{T} = 1/4\,\text{h}$

44. $1111_{\text{base 3}} = (1)(3^3) + (1)(3^2) + (1)(3^1) + (1)(3^0) =$

    $27 + 9 + 3 + 1 = 40_{\text{base 10}}$

45. $24_{\text{eight}} + 15_{\text{eight}} + 12_{\text{eight}} = 51_{\text{eight}} = (5)(8) + (1)(8^0) = 43_{\text{ten}}$

———

BASIC FUNDAMENTALS OF INTERVIEWING

TABLE OF CONTENTS

	Page
INSTRUCTIONAL OBJECTIVES	1
CONTENT	1
INTRODUCTION	1
1. Before the Interview Starts	1
Reasons for Interviews	1
Completing Applications or Forms	2
2. Conducting Interviews	2
Starting the Interview	2
Importance of Understanding People	3
Guiding the Body of the Interview	3
Related Factors	3
Purpose of Interview	3
Closing the Interview	4
Remembering Key Points	4
Problems in Interviewing	4
3. After the Interview	6
Evaluating the Interview	6
Checking References	7
Obtaining Information from References	7
STUDENT LEARNING ACTIVITIES	8
TEACHER MANAGEMENT ACTIVITIES	8
EVALUATION QUESTIONS	9
Answer Key	11

BASIC FUNDAMENTALS OF INTERVIEWING

INSTRUCTIONAL OBJECTIVES

1. Ability of the public-service employee to work toward becoming a good interviewer or interviewee on his job and in his life
2. Ability to conduct referral or other interviews to obtain and verify information
3. Ability to observe interviewees skillfully
4. Ability to evaluate the effectiveness of an interview
5. Ability to cope with problems that come up during an interview
6. Ability to check an applicant's references

CONTENT

INTRODUCTION

This unit is designed to develop the student's ability to interview people, and to obtain and verify information. It will also give trainees practice in special-purpose interviews, such as making referrals, classifying prohibited behavior, protective intervention, employment, financial eligibility, etc.

Public-service workers will be required to give different kinds of interviews on various occasions. They may be required to interview other professional personnel in their major occupational group and to grant interviews to official personnel. They will certainly be interviewed at some time for such things as jobs, raises, credit ratings, and opening bank accounts. Certain public-service workers will also be required to interview clients, patients, pupils, families, etc.

For the majority of the students, the role of an interviewer will be a new one. In the past, some of them have been the unwilling, nervous, perhaps hostile recipients of interviews by welfare workers, police, and employers. Practice interviews, relative to their future jobs, can serve as a base for proficiency in interviewing skills.

Students should acquire necessary theory and skills to become aware of the various kinds of interviews and the people who conduct them. Various types of interviews include: employment, counseling, newspaper reporting and police interrogation. Interviews are performed by a wide variety of people: psychologists, social-service workers, lawyers, salesmen, policemen, tax inspectors, immigration officers, journalists, and many more.

1. BEFORE THE INTERVIEW STARTS

Reasons for Interviews: The kind of interview depends basically on its reason – some give advice, some seek information, some give information. Here are some of the major reasons for conducting an interview:
- To obtain information
- To evaluate a person's background
- To evaluate the interviewee's character and/or personality

- To provide information
- To maintain good public or employee relations

<u>Completing Applications or Forms</u>: Another major reason for conducting an interview is to help the public or coworkers in filling out applications or forms. In this kind of interview one needs to assist the interviewee in clarifying needed information or in filling in the form correctly. Since needed information can easily be omitted, the forms must be checked for completeness.

If a form is to be used for a later interview, the interviewer may want to prepare questions from the information furnished. Areas to look for in this case include:
- Identifying factors needing elaboration
- Identifying factors that will bring out more information
- Identifying factors that are not clear

In reviewing applications or forms, there are certain critical areas to watch for, such as an interviewee's work experience. The applicant's work experience should contain sufficient details in these areas:

- Amounts of time
- Types of work experience
- Financial levels of compensation

These three factors are usually given great weight in evaluating the applicant. Other important areas to watch include the applicant's financial ability, and his prior credit references. Age should be taken into account when checking credit references. A young man or woman, for example, should not be expected to have established an extensive credit rating.

2. CONDUCTING INTERVIEWS

An interview is essentially an interaction between people through words and acts. During this process, knowledge is acquired by both interviewer and interviewee.

It is important to note that the information sought should be purposeful and related to the reason for the interview. A license interviewer should not be primarily concerned with attempting to classify whether the interviewee's behavior requires intervention from the law enforcement agencies. Common sense should dictate that the kinds of questions asked should be determined by the "role" of the agency, and the immediate concerns of the person being interviewed.

<u>Starting the Interview</u>: One of the first tasks in the beginning of an interview is the establishment of rapport, or mutual liking or respect. After a friendly atmosphere has been created by putting the applicant at ease, the interviewer can ask the first question. If the interview has to do with a specific application, the interviewer should pick non-controversial matter from the form to discuss first. Use of these techniques is designed to get the applicant talking. An atmosphere should be created that will encourage the interviewee to discuss freely what is on his mind.

Importance of Understanding People: The interviewer should have a good knowledge of human behavior and interpersonal relationships. He should realize that people often behave in an inconsistent way. They may give themselves away in an interview by saying one thing orally, and by expressing the opposite meaning in body movements.

The interviewer should be able to observe applicants skillfully. The responsibility of utilizing all the senses to obtain and mentally verify information received during the interview occurs daily on the job. The successful social-service worker, for example, must master these techniques quickly in order to improve his effectiveness.

Guiding the Body of the Interview: Ask questions to get information. There are basically two kinds of questions: *directive* and *nondirective*.

The *directive question,* as its name implies, guides or directs the interviewee in a specific area. Directive questions can usually be answered with a few words, such as "yes" or "no." A typical directive question might be, "How long have you worked at the XYZ Company?"

Nondirective questions, on the other hand, give the interviewee a chance to say what is on his mind. Words such as *what, how,* and *why* are often used in nondirective questioning. A typical nondirective question might be, "Why did you leave the XYZ Company, Mr. Rean?"

A good technique to use to encourage the applicant to talk is to begin with a nondirective question. If the applicant does not respond appropriately to a nondirective question, then use a more directive question. An example of this technique could be:

Interviewer: *What did you dislike most about your last job?*
Interviewee: *Oh, not much.*
Interviewer: *Did you feel as though your supervisor treated you fairly?*
Interviewee: *My supervisor! That guy was definitely not fair – let me tell you...*

In the above simplified example one can see how the interviewer began with a general question about the job, and when he felt that the applicant didn't respond appropriately, he used a more specific directive question, which in this case triggered a response from the applicant. By alternating between directive and nondirective questions, an interviewer can skillfully guide the discussion and obtain the necessary information from the interviewee.

Related Factors: Factors that will affect the relationship in the interview can either help or hinder the process. These will strengthen the relationship: interest, demonstrated concern, attentiveness, willingness to listen, and questioning for fuller understanding of issues at hand. On the other hand, there are some factors which obstruct relationships, such as indifference, judgmental attitudes, insensitivity, being aloof, inactivity, or being late for appointments.

Purpose of Interview: If the purpose of the interview is to help the interviewee, the interviewer should be *supportive,* and exhibit a positive and active understanding of feelings which are given expression by his behavior. However, if the interview is designed to be an interrogation of a prisoner, the method of its conduct is determined by many factors: suspect, crime, time element, and location (field, home, or headquarters).

Techniques and methods of police interrogation have had to change in recent years, and the police must now be more aware of protecting each citizen's private rights. Each suspect should be advised of his rights before his statement will be considered admissible for evidence. Citizens must not be arbitrarily subjected to interrogation; the officer must have more than just a hunch, and must be able to substantiate his reason for an interrogation. However, if an officer has good reason to be suspicious, whatever the reasons may be, he has a duty to make the inquiry or interrogation.

As can be seen, the purpose of the interview can have a drastic effect on guiding the body of the interview.

Closing the Interview: In terminating the interview, the interviewee should be told when he can expect a decision or obtain the necessary information he needs. If possible, the interviewer should answer any final questions the applicant may have.

If the applicant has to be rejected, the interviewer should accomplish this diplomatically. Courtesy and tact are especially important at this point in the interview, if a good image of the interviewer's agency is to be projected to the public.

If the interview had definite time limits, it is a good idea to remind the applicant at the beginning of this fact, and once again a few minutes before the time is up, to give the interviewee a chance to conclude his discourse.

Remembering Key Points: An effective technique for the interviewer to use during the interview is to take notes. This will help him to remember the main points of the conversation. On some occasions, however, taking notes during the course of an interview can be distracting to the applicant, or can sometimes inhibit the interviewee's responsiveness. In such cases, the interviewer should write his notes immediately after the interview. The applicant will not then be distracted, and the interviewer can remember the key points of the discussion while they are still fresh in his mind.

Problems in Interviewing: A major difficulty in interviewing involves dealing with *ambivalence* (feelings of simultaneous attraction and repulsion) and sometimes, open conflict. The interviewer should become aware of these types of applicant behavior:

- The person asks for advice, but doesn't use it
- The person agrees to a plan, but doesn't carry it out
- The person says one thing, and does another

Does this ambivalence exist in only the interviewee, or does it also exist in the interviewer? In fact, the degree to which the interviewer understands himself and is aware of his own feelings has a direct effect on the conduct of the interview. Problem areas to explore include:

- *The feelings of the Interviewer* – Do they interfere in an interview? What forms of expression do they take? Is control of one's own feelings important? Why?
- *Over-involvement by the Interviewer* – Is this helpful or harmful? What kinds of behavior might result from a non-professional approach to interviewing?

Prejudice: If the interviewer is rigid and inflexible in his thinking, this could have a harmful impact on the interview. The goal of the interviewer should be to become aware of his personal biases, and honestly try to control them, so that the interview can be conducted in a fair and honest way.

Confidentiality: A public office is, in many ways, a public trust. As an interviewer, one should become familiar with the extent to which confidential information is shared by other people in his agency. The procedures for sharing confidential information should be known, and a clear definition should be given at each agency as to what constitutes confidential information. Whenever information of a confidential nature must be shared with others, it should be on a need-to-know basis, and its confidentiality should be carefully explained to the person receiving the information.

Dependence, Interdependence and Independence:

- How are the qualities of dependence, interdependence and independence manifested in the interview? To some extent, these characteristics exist in all people.
- Are these qualities good or bad, or does it depend upon the circumstances?

For example, a positive aspect of dependence is the ability to trust and form deep personal relationships. A negative aspect of being overly dependent is the resultant lack of self-reliance and initiative. People who are independent are usually self-confident; however, too much independence could be a problem in the interviewing process. Interdependence among individuals can be seen in marriages, working relationships, and in interviewing. Examples of group interdependences include:

- Between agencies
- Between agencies and the community, and
- Between local, state and federal governmental agencies

Undue Hurry When Questioning Applicants:

- Don't anticipate what the interviewee is going to say. It's easy to jump to conclusions; much harder to hold one's judgment.
- Another habit to avoid is putting words in the applicant's mouth.
- Don't let the applicant lead you astray in the interview.
- Get the interviewee back on the track by acknowledging his remark, and asking a directive question back on the main point of the discussion.

Controlling the Interview: The extent to which the interviewer feels a need to control the interview will, of course, be determined by the purpose of the interview. Much less control would be exerted on an interviewee in a social-service agency than in a law enforcement agency while interrogating a suspect.

Shy applicants should be encouraged to open up by asking them non-directive or open-ended questions. An overly talkative applicant can be controlled by asking more directive questions, and by watching for digressions during the discussion.

Common Weaknesses of Interviewers: Here are some of the more common faults of interviewers:

- *Talking too much* – especially in those interviews that are designed to get information from the interviewee.
- *Guiding applicant too much* – particularly in those interviews that are designed to allow the interviewee to express whatever is troubling him.
- *Dominating the interview* – it should be a process of give and take.
- *Talking down to the applicant* – this condescending attitude can usually be spotted pretty easily.
- *Failing to listen* – a common fault, however, inexcusable for an interviewer.

3. AFTER THE INTERVIEW

Evaluating the Interview

- What information was learned about the applicant?
- Was it sufficient?
- What was not learned that should have been?
- If problems came up in the interview, who made the decisions?
- What was the role of the interviewer and interviewee?

Some of the factors involved in decision-making are:

- Facts involved – how are they maintained?
- Availability of acceptable alternatives
- Readiness to take action

There are definite dangers to be aware of when making decisions or evaluating an interviewee. One such danger is irrational prejudice. Each of us is biased to a certain extent, either for or against certain ethnic, racial, or religious groups. The better the interviewer understands himself, and in particular the more he is aware of his personal beliefs towards certain individuals and groups, the better off he will be for having recognized them. He can then compensate for any prejudicial bias.

This bias could work in the opposite manner. For example, an interviewer could be so blinded by an applicant's good traits, that he would not see his faults because of this *halo effect*.

Checking References: A part of the process of many interviews involves the actual checking of personal references for these purposes:

- To verify information obtained from the application and interview
- To obtain an evaluation by people who know the interviewee's work history
- To obtain additional information not disclosed on the application or during the interview

Additional verifying information may be obtained from letters of reference supplied by the applicant. There are some disadvantages to letters of reference. They may be vague or even dishonest. Sometimes, such letters may not contain the information sought. Quite often, information supplied directly by the applicant's past employers is the best source to use. When evaluating replies, consider these factors:

- They may not be complete
- They may be vague to cover negative factors
- They may contain information taken from records which may not tell the complete story

Obtaining Information from References: Letter writing is a standard way of obtaining information about an individual. However since a letter may take too much time, or cost too much, it is recommended that the telephone should be used whenever possible. One reason for the telephone's effectiveness is that a direct contact with the reference is possible. This makes for better communication, since specific questions and follow-up answers can be obtained. In addition, doubts and omissions can be picked up from the person's voice.

Before making a telephone call to a reference, a checklist of questions should first be prepared. In talking to the reference, the following guidelines should be utilized.

- Establish rapport
- Be businesslike
- Let reference talk freely
- Don't put words in respondent's mouth
- Probe for strengths and weaknesses

A personal visit is sometimes advantageous, and can often be more effective in bringing out more information about the applicant. In such cases, arrange to meet the reference and use the same principles as in the telephone checks.

Finally, information may be obtained concerning references by the hiring of outside investigators. This method has the advantages of getting more personal and more objective information. There are, however certain disadvantages: the outside investigator may not obtain the best available information, and there may be considerable expense involved.

STUDENT LEARNING ACTIVITIES

- Participate in role-playing exercises after being given a brief introduction to the basic techniques of interviewing.
- Role-play in a wide variety of interviews, such as employment, welfare eligibility, and license application, and gain experience as both an interviewer and interviewee.
- Observe interviews during role-playing exercises, evaluating what the interviewee is communicating.
- Listen to examples of interviews on tape, and be prepared to discuss the techniques used to overcome problems that developed during the interview.
- Interview public-service workers in your community about their jobs to learn more about careers, and practice newly acquired interviewing skills.
- Write a short essay on how to conduct an interview. Include the start, guidance, conclusion, and evaluation of the results.
- Talk to public-service employees who do a great deal of interviewing in their jobs. Be prepared to discuss questions with them.
- Talk to your school guidance counselor or psychologist about interviewing skills.

TEACHER MANAGEMENT ACTIVITIES

- Plan on utilizing role-playing exercises to practice knowledge learned.
- Have students play both the interviewer and interviewee in various types of interviews, such as eligibility, employment, license interviews, etc.
- Prepare tapes of different types of interviews, and play them for the class to discuss and evaluate.
- Encourage students to use all their senses as interviewers to carefully observe what is being communicated by the interviewee.
- Encourage individual practice of interviewing skills whenever possible, such as with local public-service employees.
- Assign short essays on the process of interviewing: starting, guiding, concluding, and evaluating.
- Obtain specialized interviewing materials, such as public-safety techniques from neighboring police departments.
- Arrange to have public service workers come into the class to talk about interviewing techniques.
- Provide opportunities for the school guidance counselor or psychologist to discuss interviewing skills.
- Approach the theory of interviewing through practice situations whenever possible.
- Borrow interviewing films from the local library or educational resource center.

Evaluation Questions
Interviewing Skills

1. The purpose of an interview could be:
    A. To obtain information
    B. To give information
    C. To evaluate a person's background
    D. All of the above

    1._____

2. The first job of the interview is to:
    A. Get to the subject quickly
    B. Put the applicant at ease
    C. Tell the applicant about the boss
    D. Tell the applicant about the job that is open

    2._____

3. A skillful interview will:
    A. Watch the applicant's body language
    B. Listen to the applicant
    C. Ask questions to get information
    D. All of the above

    3._____

4. Questions that are specific and can be answered "yes" or "no" are:
    A. Directive
    B. Non-directive
    C. Indirective
    D. None of the above

    4._____

5. If the applicant cannot be hired, the interview should:
    A. Avoid telling the applicant
    B. Tell the applicant as bluntly as possible
    C. Tell the applicant tactfully
    D. Give the applicant another chance

    5._____

6. Taking notes during an interview can:
    A. Help the interviewer remember the main points
    B. Be distracting to the interviewee
    C. Make the interviewee reluctant to talk
    D. All of the above

    6._____

7. An interviewer with personal likes and dislikes should:
    A. Try to control them in order to be flexible
    B. Try to find people with the same likes and dislikes
    C. Try to get rid of all personal likes and dislikes
    D. None of the above

    7._____

8. The telephone is an effective way of finding information because   8._____
    A. Doubts can be picked up from a person's voice
    B. The person called can talk freely
    C. It doesn't take much time
    D. All of the above

9. Interviewers should: 9._____
    A. Reach conclusions about the applicant as soon as possible
    B. Keep applicants on track by asking directive questions
    C. Let applicants talk on any subject comfortable to them
    D. Help with words when the applicant is unable to think

10. Shy applicants may talk more if the interviewer: 10._____
    A. Looks bored
    B. Asks open-ended questions
    C. Asks directive questions
    D. Does most of the talking

11. Interviewers should: 11._____
    A. Talk down to the applicant
    B. Make sure they dominate the interview
    C. Listen as well as talk
    D. Guide the applicant's words

12. After interviews, interviewers should ask themselves: 12._____
    A. What was learned about the applicant?
    B. What was not learned?
    C. What problems came up and if they were solved?
    D. All of the above

13. Which one is not a reason for asking for personal references?   13._____
    A. To find out information about the applicant's family
    B. To find what people who know the applicant think of their work
    C. To find out if the information on the application is true
    D. To get more information

14. Letters of reference may be: 14._____
    A. Incomplete
    B. Vague
    C. Dishonest
    D. All of the above

15. Information told in confidence should: 15._____
    A. Not be kept from all office personnel
    B. Not be told to anyone
    C. Be told to those who need-to-know
    D. None of the above

KEY (CORRECT ANSWERS)

1. D	6. D	11. C
2. B	7. A	12. D
3. D	8. D	13. A
4. A	9. B	14. D
5. C	10. B	15. C

TECHNIQUES OF DECISION MAKING

CONTENTS

INSTRUCTIONAL OBJECTIVES		1
CONTENT		1
Introduction		1
1. What is Decision Making?		
2. A Formula for Decision Making		2
A. Isolate the Problem		3
What Is the Real Problem?		
What Are the Problems?		
What Are the Symptoms?		
B. Analyze the Facts		5
How Many Facts Should be Gathered?		
Where Are the Needed Facts Obtained?		
C. Organizing the Facts		7
Grouping the Facts		
Cost		
Time		
Past Precedent		
Procedure		
Leadership		
Quality		
Productivity		
D. Stating the Real Problem		9
Is There a Real Problem or Just Symptoms?		
What Objective Is To Be Achieved?		
E. Developing Alternative Solutions		10
Present All Alternatives for Consideration		
List the Alternatives		
F. Selecting the Best Alternative Solution		11
List the Consequences of the Decision		
Be a Devil's Advocate		
Scrutinize the Final Alternatives Thoroughly		
Involve Your Superiors		
G. Implement the Decision		13
3. Summation		13
STUDENT LEARNING ACTIVITIES		14
TEACHER MANAGEMENT ACTIVITIES		15
EVALUATION QUESTIONS		17

TECHNIQUES OF DECISION MAKING

INSTRUCTIONAL OBJECTIVES
1. Ability to define decision making.
2. Ability to learn the decision-making formula.
3. Ability to learn how to state problems simply and accurately.
4. Ability to determine the difference between a symptom and a cause.
5. Ability to determine which facts are most important to a decision.
6. Ability to be able to qualify information according to importance and subject classification.
7. Ability to learn to identify two or more alternative solutions for a problem.
8. Ability to develop an openness to creative ideas.
9. Ability to learn to weigh the consequences of alternative decisions.
10. Ability to select and justify the most appropriate decision.

CONTENT

INTRODUCTION

Every person, each day, is faced by numerous situations which require the making of many decisions throughout the course of the day. It is necessary to answer such questions as: *When do I get up in the morning? What clothes will I wear? What will I have for breakfast? Which route will I take to school?*

Working in the field of public service, an individual is constantly faced with a series of situations which require him to take some particular course of action. Many such actions may not require special decision making on his part, because his particular organization has provided ways for him to make these decisions rather automatically. For example, there are department policies, and standard ways of performing certain jobs. A person also has his own past experiences of success which enable him to easily make certain decisions for such things as: the hours he should work, his rate of pay, and the required forms which must be completed for certain kinds of activities. All of these things are handled rather automatically on the job, because people have methods of handling certain things in certain ways. These become habit. They fit within a regular pattern.

There are many situations faced by a decision maker where the consequences of his action are so minor that it doesn't really matter which way he decides to solve a given problem as long as it is resolved: for example, what pencil to choose; the color of the paper on a final report; the diverting of automobiles during a traffic jam.

However, there are also other situations where the way a manager or supervisor solves a problem has great impact on an organization. Sometimes a person doesn't have a chance to actually know what is right and what is wrong. Judgment might have no well established basis. The opportunity to select between two alternatives of equal value does not exist. The situation is not clearcut. It requires thought and careful judgment; it has far-reaching consequences on the organization-affecting the quality of service, costs, schedules, the relationships between people in a working unit. Appropriate action must be taken in such assorted areas as overtime, employee dismissal, grievances, types of equipment to purchase, ways to reduce waste. The effectiveness and efficiency of the decision-making process of one individual can have far-reaching impact on a public-service organization.

Good decisions allow individuals to control and monitor their operations. Bad ones can cause worse problems and hinder the effectiveness of an organization. Things just don't happen by chance. They are made to happen. They are arranged. They can quite often be developed over a period of time which has been required by the nature of the problem or activity.

1. <u>WHAT IS DECISION MAKING?</u>

Decision making involves a conscious choice or selection of one behavior alternative from a group of two or more behavior alternatives.

Thus, there are two basic elements in a decision-making process: one, the matter of conscious choice, and the other of alternatives. *To decide, then, really means to cut off, to come to a conclusion, to end.*

2. <u>*A FORMULA FOR DECISION MAKING*</u>

Decision-making is a skill that can be developed. One way in which it can be developed is through a formula, a procedure which provides a formal process or system involving the basic rules of decision-making. There are no born decision makers, but some people appear to act very efficiently on the basis of hunches. These people may never be seen with charts and graphs, or performing a lot of analytical tasks. However, they've probably developed their own way of sifting facts and of solving problems. Good decision makers usually know their personnel; have prior experience; they can put together difficult possibilities quickly. They have their own personal *formulas* of decision making.

An effective technique to help make decisions is through the aid of a formula — a kind of check-off list to help find answers to difficult situations, to resolve problems, to handle unique situations. Such a formula enables one to take advantage of his past experiences, to see the whole picture, and to utilize all the facts he can find which are applicable to the solution.

A decision-making formula worthy of our consideration has six steps:

- *Isolate* - State the apparent problem or situation with which you plan to deal.

- *Analyze* - Gather the facts.

- *Diagnose* - Organize and interpret the facts.

- *Prescribe procedures* - State the <u>real</u> problem or situation.

- *Implement procedures* - Develop alternative solutions.

- *Evaluate* - Select the most appropriate alternative. <u>Decide.</u>

We will consider each of these steps separately. However, it should be kept in mind that these separate steps are really all related and part of the whole process of decision making.

A. *Isolate the Problem*. A problem can be a situation, question, matter, or person that is perplexing or difficult, that obstructs the way to achieving a goal or objective.

Almost everyone has problems: students have study problems when they don't know answers to test questions; people have money problems when they can't pay all of their bills. Individuals have problems with people who are unfriendly; problems with their girlfriends or boyfriends; growth problems; health problems; psychological problems.

There are professionals and specialists to whom people can go with their problems. A person takes his malfunctioning car to a mechanic, he calls on the plumber to fix leaky pipes, contacts the doctor when he doesn't feel well. These specialists are skilled problem solvers in a particular area. They have had special training and experience. They may even have had to pass examinations to obtain certificates or licenses.

In decision making, one must recognize problems as well as symptoms of problems. It is particularly important to be able to separate symptoms from causes.

What is the Real Problem? Problems are often presented in very broad terms: "Gee, John, they've really fouled up in accounting. Go straighten them out." "Boy, do we have a morale problem." "We have to introduce that new system right away." "Those two managers just don't get along."

Consider the question of morale, for example. Is morale really the **problem**, or is it more accurately the symptom of another problem? Chances **are** that it is a symptom of a problem rather than the real problem itself. The problem situation might be poor organizational structure, bad working conditions, an unfriendly supervisor, unfair treatment, or a number of other difficulties.

To help in determining what is a symptom and what is a cause, several questions must be asked:

- *"How else might the problem be stated?"* The placement of accountants in one isolated department, without the opportunity to discuss actual income and outgo with supervisors, has given us unrealistic budget figures.

  The lack of adding machines, a broken calculator, dim light, uncomfortable room temperatures, and individual working spaces has caused a greater number of absences.

  The accounting manager has openly criticized senior staff members in front of their fellow workers.

  The department secretaries were all forced to work overtime for staying five minutes past their lunch hours.

- *"What else is involved?"*

  If there are no communications between accountants and supervisors, neither group will know the reasons behind the requests or needs of the others.

  There has been talk about a computer eliminating some of the accounting jobs.

  The senior accountants have been slow to pick up the new accounting procedures.

  This is the tenth time this month that the financial unit has been unable to take care of the people in line because the secretaries were not here.

- *"Are there similar problems in other departments?"*

  The people in supplies have been ordering the wrong equipment.

  There have been layoffs in several departments.

  Several department managers are competing for the job of assistant director of our organization.

  None of the other departments have problems with secretaries.

- *"Is this a problem or a symptom?"*

    The real problem is that the accountants have not been properly informed of the organizational structure, and thus have very poor understanding of the departments which comprise the organization.

    Another organization nearby has announced opportunities for accountants at higher pay, and in new offices.

    The accounting manager and his senior staff do not plan departmental modifications together.

    Only one of the secretaries has a watch and it is five minutes slow. They play bridge at lunch time several days each month.

- *"How do others perceive the problem?"*

    Talk to all the accountants and managers individually.

    Talk to personnel about accounting re-classification.

    Interview the senior staff.

Visit with the secretaries.

<u>What are the Problems? What are the Symptoms?</u> If your automobile won't start, it might not be because it's old, the engine is dirty, or your windshield wipers don't work the car may be out of gas. It might, however, be time to give it some other attention, too. If you can recognize the symptoms, you can avoid a lot of problems.

B. <u>Analyze the Facts.</u> When the problem is recognized, then all the facts required for a successful decision can, and should be accumulated. Too often, people think they have all the facts, but they don't. It's like trying to put together a jigsaw puzzle, and recognizing, after many frustrating hours, that six pieces are missing.

Frequently, the decision maker feels that because he is in a particular situation, he knows it better than anyone else can know it. The issue may, therefore, be somewhat clouded. This cloudiness may prevent him from seeing what is actually there.

How many times have individuals had to make a decision and found that they didn't have the right facts or sufficient quantities of facts to insure a good decision? Both the quality and effectiveness of most decisions can be seriously reduced without good facts.

When gathering facts, one should write them down, and gather them into one comprehensive list. The decision maker can then visualize them all at the same time, and is much less likely to overlook or forget any of them. In dealing with large amounts of information, he can grade sub-topics and keep track of them in a systematic way.

How many facts should be gathered? The number usually depends on the nature and complexity of the situation.

Basically it means that the amount of information accumulated depends upon such factors as:

- The amount of time available.

- Is it an emergency situation or not?

- The seriousness of the situation.

- The availability of information, etc.

Where are the Needed Facts Obtained?

- First, he might turn to available records. He usually has financial records, personal records, records of transactions, and records of activities.

- Second, he may have references: newspapers, journals, old letters, the like.

- Third, and very importantly, he has other people, or he has a staff. There is a great deal of expertise within most public-service organizations: specialists in economics, human relations, law, health, safety, and other areas; all responsive to the request of the decision-maker. An outside expert, or consultant, may be required in difficult situations.

- Finally, look at other organizational units which have been confronted with similar problems. Quite often, through investigation, the decision-maker finds that precedents have been set which he may have to follow. In law, for example, he may have to base a decis.ion on the verdict of a case held on the same issue, long ago in a distant place.

Sources of information are unlimited. It takes a great deal of initiative to uncover them.

How should the facts be obtained? Here again, there are questions we must ask ourselves:

- What kinds of facts are available?

- What information is available?

- Is there enough?

- Is help needed, and where can it be obtained?

- Who else might have the information needed?

Going back to the morale problem, which was found to be the result of a basic lack of communication between accountants and departmental managers, how might the decision-maker proceed?

In gathering the facts, he would have to obtain both the accountant's records and the manager's records. The decision-maker might call upon organizations of similar size and activity, to see how they handle difficulties of this nature. He might talk to one or more senior accountants in a large public accounting firm or contact the governmental auditors. He might even write letters to colleagues seeking their advice.

The decision-maker might hold a meeting of selected members of his staff, or assign a task force of accountants and managers to look into the matter.

As he begins to gather his facts, the decision-maker will discover that other information is required. Additionally, he will uncover sources of other facts. The quality of the facts he gathers ultimately affects the quality of his decisions. The better the data, the better the opportunity to make a good decision.

C. <u>Organizing the Facts.</u> Once the facts have been collected, it becomes very important that they be organized to help the decision-maker interpret what they really mean. To do this, it's helpful to set them up in categories -- to pull like items together.

This procedure helps people to know whether certain facts are more important than others, and thus deserve special consideration.

Grouping the Facts. There are several categories into which information can be grouped, such as: cost, time, past precedent, procedures, leadership, quality, and productivity:

Cost. In cost considerations, one must look at unit costs, personnel costs, material costs, equipment costs, mailing costs, etc. If, for example, an individual is attempting to determine the cost of mailing out new contracts to several hundred vendors with whom the agency deals, the following costs may have to be considered, among others:

- *Duplication costs per duplicated copy.*

- *Salary costs of writing new contract.*

- *Salary costs of typing contracts.*

- *Costs of new contract forms.*

- *Costs of envelopes.*

- *Costs of writing departmental letters.*

Time. Time is usually calculated in terms of the personnel costs or salaries paid. The basic periods of time hours, days, weeks, months, years are quite often combined in terms of man-hours, man-weeks, man-years, etc., to enable the numbers of hour units to be multiplied by salary allocations. Equipment time, particularly in this age of computers, can be quite expensive.

Past Precedent. This is a category relating together data on similar situations in the past, and to consider the decisions arrived at in those situations for their bearing on the decision to be made in the present.

Procedures. These are also important. Most public-service organizations have certain ways of accomplishing functions or providing services. They have been proven over a period of time to be most appropriate to particular situations. Here, too, is where organizational policy making may be involved and possibly changed and modified.

Leadership. This would include the directions and decisions which brought about a particular situation, and permit review of the factors which were present when prior decisions were made.

Quality. The quality of facts is important. There must be an assurance that the right data, and the most applicable figures and information, are available.

Productivity. This category would enable a comparison between various activities which would bring about particular results. It would provide an opportunity to look at the output of a department or project team.

In pulling together like items, one can see trends, certain facts which may be more important than others, and areas where there are gaps in the information.

In organizing facts, the following questions should be asked:

- Which facts are related to each other?

- Are these facts related to any not listed?

- What is the extent of their relationship?

- Are they relevant to this situation?

- What is the level of reliability of the facts?

- Can the problem be more clearly defined with the information listed?

- How can it be done?

- How much time is there for further organization?

- Are these facts recurring or one time events?

D. *Stating the Real Problem*. Having examined the data, the decision-maker is now in a position to state the *real* problem or situation with which he has to deal. He now knows whether he has a problem, or just a misunderstanding. Was the original statement just a symptom, or was it a real situation? It might be that there are several problems. Whatever the situation, it must be stated in clear and simple terms. It should be written down.

A problem is a situation which deviates from an expected standard, or norm of desired performance. In decision making, one starts with an *apparent* problem. The decision maker gathers more information in order to more accurately identify the situation with which he is going to deal.

Is there a real problem? or just symptoms? The data have been gathered and organized. Now it is necessary to zero in on the actual situation, and to see whether there is a real problem. Was the initial identification a symptom of a problem, or was it a real cause? Is there one problem, or several?

If the decision-maker neglected to gather the facts, and then to organize, analyze, and categorize them, he might find himself working on the wrong situation. He could spend a great deal of time and effort on symptoms, and could actually be working on the wrong problem. Certainly, he could overlook a number of relevant factors.

If a medical doctor spent all of his time studying symptoms, he might be too late to address an actual problem and his patient could die. Similarly, in a public-service organization, *if too much time and energy is spent in chasing symptoms instead of causes, problems can become crises.*

What objective is to be achieved? Remember, one must still think about decision making in terms of fulfilling objectives.

When it is known what kind of performance should be achieved, and what kind of performance has been received, the necessary effort is simple merely to measure the difference between those two points. The decision-maker must identify the deviation and its extent. He will also have to specifically state the standard, or *norm,* toward which he is trying to return.

In other words, not only does he have to state the problem to which he is going to address himself, but he must specifically state the objective he wants to achieve.

In the previous illustration of the public-service organization and the communication problems between the accountants and managers, the objectives could, perhaps, be restated in this manner: *it is necessary to design a realistic and accurate budget for costs.*

This stage would complete the problem identification part of the decision-making process. Now, he can get on with decision-making itself.

E. *Developing Alternative Solutions*. With the *real* problem determined and stated, the decision-maker is now in a position to begin the development of alternative solutions. Notice that there is an "s" on the end of "solution." Decision-makers should be interested in as many solutions to a problem as can be developed.

This particular phase of the decision making process should be very free-wheeling. It should produce a number of ideas. The decision-maker should keep his mind open. He should not be too judgmental, but should avoid premature criticism. *Criticism given too early can destroy new ideas that could be beneficial.*

Picture a staff meeting, where the assistant director of the agency presents an entirely new approach to providing recreational opportunities for senior citizens. He is interrupted by his superior, the director, who tells him that his idea is ridiculous. It is unlikely that he would ever bring up the subject again unless he were extremely persistent and unafraid of the director. *Creative thinking can be squelched by a superior who criticizes without having much of a basis for criticism.*

The number of alternatives that can be developed at any one point in time is a function of how much time is spent in developing these alternatives. It's always helpful to stop and ask: "If I didn't have any rules to follow in this organization, would I handle the situation any differently?" Or, "What else could I do?" Perhaps it is desirable to modify several previously stated alternatives to produce one better alternative.

Present all alternatives for consideration. By considering all ideas as initially feasible, they can be brought out into the open. Such occasions are often called brain storming sessions. Regardless of how silly an idea might seem at first, perhaps when it is considered in the light of other possibilities it may turn out to be a fairly useable solution; or maybe a portion of that idea might be able to be combined with another idea and thereby produce the ultimate solution.

What, for example, would have happened if someone stifled the idea of the paper clip? "Isn't that stupid, who'd want to hold pieces of paper together with bent up wire?" Evidently, people laughed at Columbus, and his idea of a round world; they laughed at John Fulton and his steamship; and even at a young man named Fosbury, who high-jumped backwards. Regardless of ridicule, however, each of these men, in his solution to the problem at hand, succeeded in his particular project.

How many people have been shot-down in creative projects, by comments such as these: "We've tried it and it didn't work," "That's against policy," "It would cost too much," "He hasn't got the experience," "He"s too young."

List the Alternatives. Looking at the positive side of the argument, there should be positive consideration of all methods, objects, and persons available, to satisfy the needs of decision-making. Once again, write down all of the alternatives, so that they can be comprehensively considered.

To do this, one can list all of the alternatives across the top of a chart and then systematically consider all the factors under each alternative. This chart, or *matrix,* as it is called, can then be used to evaluate the best solution.

As an example, let us assume legislation is passed in each state to award home and business loans and educational benefits to veterans of the Vietnam war. Then a matrix somewhat like this can be made:

	ALTERNATIVES					
	#1	#2	#3	#4	#5
Staff involved					
Labor costs					
Material costs					
Equipment costs					
Services included					
Services excluded					
facilities needed					
Number of veterans processed per day					
Publicity requirements					
Applicable policy					
New policies needed,					
etc.					

The list can be long, but it is well worth it. If, for example, one is considering attending a community college or university, but can't make up his mind. He can develop a chart with all of the things that are important to him on the side of the chart, and the schools under consideration acros the top. Then a five-point scale can *be* applied to each item, with five being the highest mark and zero the lowest. The school with the most points might be the most likely alternative under all the prevailing circumstances. Still, one cannot be completely definite on this basis alone, so it is necessary to move to the next step in the decision-making process, that of selection.

F. <u>Selecting the Best Alternative Solution.</u> The most important part of the decision-making process is the selection of the most appropriate alternative: *deciding.* This is the stage during which criticism is appropriate. Judgment must be made on all facets of the problem and the alternative solutions. The effectiveness of each of the solutions must be evaluated in terms of the objectives towards which the decision-maker is oriented. He must look carefully at, and criticize severely, such items as cost, timeliness, workability, acceptability, and implementation.

- Can the solution be made to work?

- Will the staff cooperate?

- Will those who are served make the necessary adjustments?

- Are there the skills in the organization to carry out the program?

<u>List the Consequences of the Decision.</u> As these and other items are considered, it is desirable to write down <u>all</u> of the consequences of <u>each</u> of the decisions. List the pro's and con's. It is not enough to add them together and make a decision on that basis, such as in the selection of a college, in the previous section. Not only does one use some type of scale, but he assigns different weights to different items. Using the previous college selection chart, the decision-maker might have to weight costs higher than the availability of co-educational dormitories, or the scholastic reputation of the school over the strength of its football team.

<u>Be a Devil's Advocate.</u> The more desirable alternatives should be scrutinized in a negative way. Take the opposite position, that is, play the *devil's advocate*. Mentally implement the plan and consider the adverse consequences.

Take one of the most favorable-looking alternatives. Ask:

- "Will it affect other departments?"

- "What could go wrong?"

- "What are the potential sources of breakdown?"

- "What new problem might it create?"

- "Where would the resistance be?"

Consider the extent to which these consequences will probably come about and the degree of seriousness of each one. Select second and even third choices in order to plan for contingencies.

<u>Scrutinize the Final Alternative Thoroughly</u>. Once the alternatives have been narrowed to only one, which appears to fill the need, then this one alternative should be subjected to one final round of positive questions:

- Will this decision fulfill the original goal?
- Can the agency live with the decision permanently?
- Is the timing of the decision right?
- Does the decision bring about the greatest benefit for the greatest number?

Involve Your Superiors. It is often necessary and desirable to go to the superiors with the decision. Ordinarily, the problem would be presented, with the attendant factors affecting it, and the alternative solutions which could resolve it. Then the decision-maker would indicate his reasons, with their consequences, for selection of the particular alternative.

G. <u>Implement the Decision.</u> After a decision is made, it must be implemented. The necessary steps must be initiated to carry it out. The whole management cycle of planning, organizing, and controlling must be brought into action, as well as other available management tools.

3. <u>SUMMATION</u>

No phase of the management cycle or any other organizational function could be carried out if decisions were not made. Planning, organizing, controlling, as well as motivating, communicating, and setting standards; these all require endless strings of decisions or choices. This is why the final process of decision making is so important.

Good decisions are the result of understanding responsibilities, involving others, knowing the organization, understanding one's own strengths and weaknesses, and being accountable for decisions made.

In understanding the responsibilities involved, one must know where to get information and be cognizant of the extent to which people can take action.

Through involving others, they gain a sense of ownership in the decision, and become more committed. They remove their defense mechanisms.

Knowing an organization requires an awareness of its organizational history and objectives, where the power centers lie, the limits of one's authority, and the way in which work is actually accomplished.

One's understanding of himself and his own shortcomings insures that he will seek out expertise he does not possess himself, and will develop ways to improve his own skills.

The individual should have this motto: *Remember, when you get right down to it, one person may have to decide – YOU!*

STUDENT LEARNING ACTIVITIES

- Prepare a definition of *decision making*.

- Write a brief paper on the decision-making formula.

- Participate in a class discussion about decision making in a selected public-service agency. Try to identify top, middle, and low-level decisions.

- Prepare a definition of the term *problem*.

- Interview a public-service official to identify a problem within his organization. Follow with a class discussion.

- Prepare a brief paper describing three examples of symptoms and their causes.

- Participate in a problem-solving case study.

- Write a brief paper on why facts must be gathered to aid in the decision-making process.

- Identify the kinds of facts and resources you must use to prepare for making decisions about a teacher-assigned topic.

- Participate in a discussion about fact finding.

- Develop with the class, and have at least 20 students complete, a survey questionnaire with open-ended questions on ways in which your school can be improved. Organize responses according to subject and year ranking of importance.

- Participate in a class discussion on the results of the questionnaire survey.

- After the class has decided on one or more ways in which the school can be improved, prepare a report on one of the objectives including:

    statement of an objective,

    facts needed and how obtained,

    categorizing the facts.

- Deliver an oral version of your report. Respond to questions and comments from the class.

- Choose five articles from the newspaper on five different topics: sports, politics, crime, etc. State the actual problem being addressed.

- Participate in a class discussion about problem identification, and problem statements. Sharpen your problem statements if necessary.

- Participate in a class discussion about problems identified and possible alternative solutions.

- Using the example of the State legislature passing a bill awarding home and business loans and educational benefits to veterans of the **Gulf War**, develop a set of alternative plans as to how the legislation may be carried out.

TEACHER MANAGEMENT ACTIVITIES

- Have students define *decision making*.

- Assign students a paper on the decision-making formula.

- Conduct a class discussion about decision-making in a selected public service agency.

- Have students prepare their own definitions of the term *problem*.

- Assign students interviews with public-service officials to identify selected organizational problems.

- Conduct a class discussion on problems in public-service organizations.

- Have students develop and discuss reports and three examples of symptoms and their causes.

- Select and assign a case study to the class in problem solving.

- Assign a paper on why facts must be gathered to aid in the decision-making process.

- Prepare a list of considerations in several public-service agencies. Have each student select one consideration around which he will gather essential facts to make a decision.

- Conduct a discussion on fact finding.

- Assign the class a survey project, entitled "How Can Our School be Improved?" Have students develop their own questionnaire and administer it to at least 20 students. Ask them to organize their results according to subject and rank of importance.

- Organize a class discussion on the results of the surveys.

- Once one or more items of possible school improvement have been agreed upon, assign the students a report to contain the following:

statement of an objective,

facts needed and how obtained,

categorizing of facts.

- Organize oral presentations of student reports.

- Assign students the reading of five articles from a newspaper on five different topics: sports, polttfcs, crime, etc. Have them state the actual problem being discussed.

- Conduct a class discussion on problem identification and problem statements.

- Assign a brief paper on the symptoms of five problems and the causes in a public service agency selected by each student.

- Conduct a class discussion on the problems and solutions identified.

- Using the example of the new bill for veterans of the Gulf War, have students develop a set of alternatives.

- Insure that the students are open to new and abstract suggestions.

- Direct oral presentations of students in which they review their original problems, the sources and categories of facts, the alternatives available for solution, their respective consequences, and their ultimate decisions. Have students challenge one another's decisions.

Evaluation Questions
Techniques of Decision Making

Read the problem carefully, and answer each of the following questions.

You are a library assistant. Mrs. Smith, the librarian, has two high school aides, Susan and Mary. Mrs. Smith has told you that she may fire Susan if her attitude does not improve. She complained about Susan's laziness and stated that Susan's work was never finished. Mrs. Smith asked you to talk to Susan about improving her attitude. When you tried to talk to Susan about this, she got upset and went home.

After observing the aides' workload for a few days, you notice that Susan has much more work than Mary.

1. What is the problem? _____

2. Name one solution. _____

3. What are the consequences of this solution? _____

4. List another solution. _____

5. What are the consequences of this solution? _____

6. Which do you think is the best solution? _____

Read the problem carefully, and answer each of the following questions.

You are in charge of the recreation program at the community center. Your job is to keep activities running smoothly. On the daily schedule, one-half hour has been set aside for basketball. While you have stepped out for a moment, ten of the Green Hornets and ten of the Purple Dragons arrived to play basketball. As each group has two teams set up, neither group would give in. Unfortunately, a fight began. The fight ended just as you returned. Each group plans to play tomorrow. You must make a decision.

1. What is the problem? _____

2. Name one solution. _____

3. What are the consequences of this solution? _____

4. List another solution. _____

5. What are the consequences of this solution? _____

6. Which do you think is the best solution? _____

Answer Key

Answers will vary on this test. The instructor may wish to have a discussion after the test, with students justifying their selections. Students may be evaluated on the soundness of their judgement.

FINDING A JOB

TABLE OF CONTENTS

	Page
INTRODUCTION	1
PLANNING YOUR TIME	2
DETERMINING YOUR JOB SKILLS	3
MATCHING YOUR BACKGROUND AND EXPERIENCE TO JOBS	4
WHERE TO GET JOB INFORMATION	4
COVER LETTERS AND APPLICATIONS	6
PREPARING YOUR RESUME	6
10 TIPS FOR THE EFFECTIVE RESUME	8
COMMON QUESTIONS ABOUT RESUMES	9
INTERVIEWING	10
COMMON QUESTIONS ABOUT INTERVIEWS	11
TESTING	13
AFTER THE INTERVIEW	14
JOB SEARCH CHECKLIST	15
MOST COMMON JOB-HUNTING MISTAKES	16
COMMON QUESTIONS ABOUT THE FOLLOW-UP	18
AFTER YOU ARE HIRED	18

FINDING A JOB

INTRODUCTION

You need a job. Somewhere, an employer has the job you want. How do you get that job? By marketing your job talents. By showing employers you have the skills they need.

Do you have job talents? Yes! Homemakers, disabled individuals, veterans, students just out of school, people already working—all have skills and experience for many good jobs.

What you need to know is how to market your talents effectively to find the right job. This guide will help you to:

- Evaluate your interests and skills
- Find job information
- Write resumes and application letters
- Prepare and plan for job interviews
- Plan your time
- Take tests

PLANNING YOUR TIME

Now is the best time to start looking for a job. You're as qualified as other applicants, so start now before someone else gets "your" job. You've already made a good start by reading this guide!

What's the most important thing to know about your job search?
<u>Finding work is a full-time job.</u>

In a full-time job, you:
* Have responsibilities (work duties and procedures)
* "Punch a clock" or be at work "on time"
* Work hard all day, 40 hours a week
* Report to a boss, who makes sure you carry out your responsibilities

To find a job, you must:
* Set your own responsibilities (things you must do every day to get a job)
* Wake up early at a set time to start looking for work
* Look hard for a job, all day, 40 hours a week
* Be your own boss (or appoint a friend to be your "boss") to make sure you carry out your job search responsibilities

Tips for Planning an Effective Job Search:

- Make a "To Do List" every day. Outline daily activities to look for a job.
- Apply for jobs early in the day. This will make a good impression and give you time to complete applications, have interviews, take tests, etc.
- Call employers to find out the best times to apply. Some companies take applications only on certain days and times during the week.
- Write down all employers you contact, the date of your contacts, people you talk to, and special notes about your contacts.
- Apply at several companies in the same area when possible. This saves time and money.
- Be prepared. Have a "master application" and resumes, pens, maps and job information with you all the time. Who knows when a "hot lead" will come your way.
- Follow up leads immediately. If you find out about a job late in the day, call right then! Don't wait until the next day.
- Network. Tell everyone you know that you're looking for a job. Stay in touch with friends and contacts. Follow up new leads immediately.
- Read pamphlets and books on how to get a job. The time you spend reading these materials will save you a lot of time in your job search.
- Make automated connections through systems on the Internet, such as America's Job Bank and the Talent Bank.

DETERMINING YOUR JOB SKILLS

Another tip for finding the right job: *Make a list of your background experience.*

If you think you don't have any experience—think again! You may not have specific job experience, but you do have work experience. You have "worked" as a homemaker, a student, a volunteer, in a hobby or some other personal activity. The skills you use for these "jobs" can be applied to other jobs.

A background and experience list may help you to fill out job applications, provide information for job interviews and prepare resumes (if you're applying for professional or office jobs).

Tips for Making a Background and Experience List:

Interests and Aptitudes
- List your hobbies, clubs you belong to, sports you're involved in, church and school activities, and things that interest you. List things you are good at or have special ability for.
- Look at the first item on your list. Think about the skills or talents it takes to do that item. Really think about it! All hobbies, activities, etc. take a lot of skills, knowledge and abilities. For example, playing basketball requires the ability to interact with others (be a "team player") and the ability to lead or direct teammates/coworkers. Homemaking requires the ability to manage budgets, handle multiple tasks and the skills to teach or train others. Fixing cars requires knowledge of electronics and machinery, and the ability to diagnose mechanical problems.

Work History
If you've worked before, list your jobs. Include volunteer, part-time, summer and self-employment. Next, write down work duties for the jobs you listed. Now think about the skills and talents it took to do each work duty. Write them down.

Education
- List the schools you attended, dates, major studies or courses completed. Include military and vocational education and on-the-job training
- List degrees, certificates, awards and honors
- Ask yourself what classes or training you like and why

Physical Condition
- Do you have any disabilities limiting the kind of work you can do? Companies will often make special accommodations to employ disabled persons (in fact, some accommodations are legally required). If you have strong or special physical capabilities, list these too.

Career Goals
- What kind of work do you want to be doing 5 or 10 years from now? What kind of job could you get now to help you reach this goal?

MATCHING YOUR BACKGROUND AND EXPERIENCE TO JOBS

Look at the abilities (talents) identified on your background and experience list. You have talents that you use every day. Now find out what jobs can use your talents.

Start at your local State Employment Service Office ("Job Service"). This office has free information about many jobs. You may be given an appointment with a career counselor who can help you decide what kind of work is best suited to your abilities and interests.

While you're at Job Service, ask to see the *Guide for Occupational Exploration* and the *Occupational Outlook Handbook* (you can also get these books at most public libraries). These easy-to-read books, published by the Department of Labor, describe work duties for different occupations, skills and abilities needed for different types of jobs, how to enter occupations, where jobs are located, training and qualifications needed, as well as earnings, working conditions and future opportunities.

Match the skills and abilities in your list to the skills and abilities of different jobs. Don't limit yourself. The important thing is not the job title, but the skills and abilities of the job. You may find that your abilities match with an occupation that you have never thought about.

WHERE TO GET JOB INFORMATION

If you know what job skills you have, you are ready to look for a job. You can look for job openings at these sources:

- Networking – Tell everyone you know you're looking for a job. Ask about openings where your friends work.
- Private employers – Contact employers directly to market your job talents. Talk to the person who would supervise you even if there are no jobs currently open.
- State Employment Service Offices provide help on finding jobs and other services, such as career counseling
- America's Job Bank – A nationwide pool of job opportunities which will extend your search to other states and can be viewed in your local Employment Service offices or on the Internet at http://www.ajb.dni.us
- Federal, state and local government personnel offices list a wide range of job opportunities. Check the government listings in your phone book.
- Local public libraries have books on occupations and often post local job announcements. Many state libraries are also providing free access to Internet through PCs.
- Newspaper ads list various job openings
- Local phone book – Look for career counseling centers in your area
- Private employment and temporary agencies offer placement (employer or job hunter may pay a fee)
- Community colleges and trade schools usually offer counseling and job information to students and the general public
- Proprietary schools – Private training centers offer instruction in specific trades (tuition is usually required). Check with your office of state education for credible schools.

- Community organizations such as clubs, associations, women and minority centers, and youth organizations
- Churches frequently operate employment services or provide job search help
- Veterans' placement centers operate through State Employment Service Offices. Veterans' social and help organizations often have job listings for members.
- Union and apprenticeship programs provide job opportunities and information. Contact your state apprenticeship council or relevant labor union directly.
- Government sponsored training programs offer direct placement or short-term training and placement for applicants who qualify. Check the yellow pages under Job Training Programs or Government Services.
- Journals and newsletters for professional or trade associations often advertise job openings in their field. Ask for these at the local library.

Under the Civil Rights Act of 1964, as amended in 1991, all of the sources listed above serve persons of any race, color, religion, sex or national origin. The Age Discrimination in Employment Act of 1967 forbids agencies to discriminate against older workers. Both laws forbid employers to discriminate in hiring.

In addition, the Americans with Disabilities Act under Title I prohibits employment discrimination against "qualified individuals with disabilities." A qualified individual with a disability is: an individual with a disability who meets the skill, experience, education and other job-related requirements of a position held or desired, and who, with or without reasonable accommodation, can perform the essential functions of a job.

MOST COMMONLY USED JOB SEARCH METHODS

Percent of Jobseekers Using this Method	Method	Effectiveness Rate
66.0%	Applied directly to employer	47.7%
50.8	Asked friends about jobs where they work	22.1
41.8	Asked friends about jobs elsewhere	11.9
28.4	Asked relatives about jobs where they work	19.3
27.3	Asked relatives about jobs elsewhere	7.4
45.9	Answered local newspaper ads	23.9
21.0	Private employment agency	24.2
12.5	School placement office	21.4
15.3	Civil Service test	12.5
10.4	Asked teacher or professor	12.1
1.6	Placed ad in local newspaper	12.9
6.0	Union hiring hall	22.2

COVER LETTERS AND APPLICATIONS

A letter of application is used when inquiring about a job or submitting an application form. If you're applying for a job that requires a resume, you should write a cover letter to accompany your resume. The purpose of these cover letters is to:
- Tell how your job talents will benefit the company
- Show why the employer should read your resume or application form
- Ask for a job interview

Tips for Writing Cover Letters
- Write a separate letter for each job application
- Type letters on quality 8 1/2" x 11" paper
- Use proper sentence structure and correct spelling and punctuation
- Convey personal interest and enthusiasm
- Keep your letter short and to the point
- Show that you've done some homework on the company (you know what they do, their interests and problems)
- Try to identify something about you that is unique or of interest to the employer
- Request an interview, and if possible, suggest a date and time
- Include your address and telephone number
- Address each letter to the specific person you want to talk to (the person who would actually supervise you)
- Highlight your job qualifications
- State the position you are seeking and the source of the job opening

PREPARING YOUR RESUME

You want to apply for a job. Do you need a resume? That depends on the kind of job you are applying for:
   * Professional, technical, administrative and managerial jobs, as well as sales, secretarial, clerical and other office jobs require a resume.
   * Skilled jobs (ex. baker, hotel clerk, electrician, drafter, welder, etc.) sometimes require a resume.
   * Unskilled, quick turnover jobs (ex. fast food server, laborers, machine loader, etc.) do not require a resume.

Tips for Good Resumes

You need two types of information to prepare your resume:
1. Self-information – You need to know your job talents, work history, education and career goals. Did you complete your background and experience list? If you did, you have the self-information required to prepare your resume.
1. Job information – Gather specific information on the job you're applying for. Here's what you need:
    - Job duties (to match your skills to the skills needed for the job). Get your job duties from the job announcement. If the announcement or ad is vague, call the employer and ask for a description of job duties.
    - Education and experience required
    - Hours and shifts usually worked

- Pay range (make their top offer the minimum acceptable!)

With the information on yourself and the job you're applying for, you're ready to write your resume.

Two Types of Resumes

Reverse Chronological – lists jobs you've had. Your most recent job is listed first, your job before that is listed second, and so on. Each job has employment dates and job duties.

Functional – describes your skills, abilities and accomplishments that relate to the job you're applying for. Employment history is less detailed than chronological resumes.

What kind of resume should you use? Answer the following questions:
- Have you progressed up a clearly defined career ladder, and you're looking for job advancement?
- Do you have recent job experience at one or more companies?

If you're answer is yes, use a reverse chronological resume.

- Are you a displaced homemaker?
- Are you a veteran and you want to relate your military training to civilian jobs?
- Do you have little or no job experience?
- Do you have gaps in your work history?
- Is the job you're applying for different from your present or recent job?
- Do you want to emphasize your work skills and accomplishments instead of describing your job duties?

If your answer to any of these is yes, use a functional resume.

Tips for Preparing a Functional Resume
- Study the duties for the job you're applying for. Identify two or three general skills that are important to the job.
- Review your background and experience list. Find talents and accomplishments that demonstrate your ability to perform the job skills.
- List your talents and accomplishments under the job skills they relate to
- Use simple, short, active sentences
- Focus attention on strong points

Tips for Preparing a Reverse Chronological Resume
- List your jobs starting with your present or most recent job. Give exact dates for each job.
- Briefly describe the main duties you performed in each job
- Emphasize duties that are important for the job you're applying for
- Use simple, short, active sentences
- Include scholarships and honors and major school subjects if related to your job goal

10 TIPS FOR THE EFFECTIVE RESUME

The following rules apply to all resumes:

1. If possible, use a computer to prepare your resume. There are computer programs that make it easy to produce a professional looking resume. Your local school, library, Employment Service local office or "quick print" shop can help.
1. Do not include irrelevant personal information (age, weight, height, marital status, etc.)
1. Do not include salary and wages
1. Center or justify all headings – Don't use abbreviations
1. Be positive and identify accomplishments
1. Use action verbs
1. Be specific – Use concise sentences, keep it short (one page is best)
1. Make sure your resume "looks good" (neat and readable)
1. Proofread the master copy carefully. Have someone else proofread it also.
1. Inspect photocopies for clarity, smudges and marks

Action Verbs

Action verbs give your resume power and direction. Try to begin all skills statements with an action verb. Here is a sample of action verbs for different types of skills:

Management	Technical	Clerical	Communication
administered	assembled	arranged	arranged
analyzed	built	catalogued	addressed
coordinated	calculated	compiled	authored
developed	designed	generated	drafted
directed	operated	organized	formulated
evaluated	overhauled	processed	
improved	remodeled	persuaded	
supervised	repaired	systemized	

Creative	Financial	Helping	Research
conceptualized	administered	assessed	clarified
created	analyzed	coached	evaluated
designed	balanced	counseled	identified
established	budgeted	diagnosed	inspected
fashioned	forecast	facilitated	organized
illustrated	marketed	represented	summarized
invented	planned		
performed	projected		

The Talent Bank

Once a resume is completed, it can be fed into the Talent Bank, now available in many local Job Service offices. The Bank is an electronically searchable database of resumes or other statements of qualification from job hunters seeking employment. Those searching for jobs or new opportunities can post their resumes/qualifications to the bank. Employers search the banks to select a group of resumes for further screening.

COMMON QUESTIONS ABOUT RESUMES

What is the purpose of a resume?
To obtain an interview. This can be quite a challenge since the average resume receives only 5-7 seconds of viewing. No one is ever hired solely on the basis of how they look on paper. The resume is your promotional literature for selling yourself. It serves to whet an employer's appetite and make him or her want to know more about you.

How do I accomplish that purpose?
By providing the most relevant information in as concise a manner as possible: the most positive, impressive highlights from your past that would be applicable to the position you seek.

What's a good way to start?
Describing yourself on paper is difficult and somewhat dehumanizing. Make a list of information about yourself, set it aside and add to it later. Place the accumulated data in a format that best emphasizes your strengths and delete the least relevant information.

What's important to emphasize?
Focus on what you have achieved and learned and not just on how and where you have spent your time. Be as specific as possible in citing examples to support your statements. Emphasize only your very best side, the information most applicable to the job at hand. Use only the most impressive tip of the iceberg that also relates to the employer's needs. Editing is difficult, but be sure not to bury the most relevant and attractive information in too much irrelevant detail.

I feel like I'm bragging.
There's no room for modesty in a job search. Employers expect to see ideal candidates, and those who don't portray themselves as such are seldom given the benefit of the doubt. Don't lie, but don't sell yourself short. Save being humble for the interview.

Is tone important in a resume?
Tone is the personality that comes through on a resume—sentence structure, word usage, etc. It can say as much about you as the content.

What is a "statement of objective?"
This is a sentence or two at the beginning of your resume that tells a prospective employer at a glance if you are a possible match for their needs. It is both general, so as to not exclude you from openings you might be interested in, yet specific, so it does communicate some boundaries to the employer. It is essential for individuals with extensive unrelated experience.

What if all my experience is unrelated to my objective?
You might want to summarize the various skills you have learned in past jobs, and emphasize the skills you've acquired that would be relevant in the prospective position. You should consider a functional resume.

What should not be included in a resume?
Information unrelated to your job objective. Also avoid using a picture, height and weight, Social Security number, and other personal information, as well as

misspelled and incorrectly used words, slang or jargon, abbreviations, and flowery or overused adjectives and phrases.

How creative should I be?

Try to be somewhat creative, but you want your resume to stand out through its content. Being overly creative with the appearance or format of the resume may turn off some employers.

What else should I know?

Standard length is one page. Avoid using "I" since this is assumed; use action verbs to describe duties and accomplishments. Use different resumes for different job types. Heavier paper gives the resume a more professional look, and be sure it is free of smudges or stray marks. Be sincere, appropriate, and keep the information relevant.

Where do I distribute the resume?

Have the resume prepared to send to all individuals you contact. You can also attach it to applications, and be sure to send a cover letter along with the resume, introducing yourself and describing your experiences to the employer. All your information should be sent to the person you have been in contact with who has the authority to hire you. Be sure to confirm spellings of names and accuracy of titles.

INTERVIEWING

Most hiring decisions are made at the first interview. How you come across in that interview could be as important as your experience and job talents. Here are some interviewing tips that will help you get the job you want:

Before the Interview
- Learn as much as you can about the company salary and benefits. Friends, neighbors and relatives who work for the company are good sources of information. Libraries, local chambers of commerce, etc. are also helpful.
- Learn everything you can about the job and how your previous experience and training qualify you for the job.
- Write down the things you will need to complete applications (background and experience list, resume or work summary, samples of work if applicable, etc.)
- Be sure to bring your social security card, driver's license, union card, military records, etc.

The Interview
- Dress for the interview as you would for the job. Don't overdress or look too informal.
- Always go to the interview alone. Arrange for babysitters, transportation and other pitfalls ahead of time so that you can be on time and relaxed in the interview.
- Find common ground with the employer. Pictures, books, plants, etc. in the employer's office can be conversation topics.
- Express your interest in the job and the company using information you gathered to prepare for the interview
- Let the interviewer direct the conversation

- Answer questions in a clear and positive manner. Show how your experience and training will make you productive in the shortest time with minimal supervision.
- Speak positively of former employers and coworkers no matter why you left even if you were fired from your last job
- Let the employer lead into conversation about benefits. Your focus on these items can be a turn off. But, don't be afraid to ask questions about things you really need to know.
- When discussing salary, be flexible—avoid naming a specific salary. If you're too high, you risk not getting the job. If you're too low, you undersell yourself. Answer questions on salary requirements with responses such as, "I'm interested in the job as a career opportunity so I'm negotiable on the starting salary." Negotiate, but don't sell yourself short.

Closing the Interview
- If the employer does not offer you a job or say when you will hear about it, ask when you may call to find out about the decision
- If the employer asks you to call or return for another interview, make a written note of the time, date and place
- Thank the employer for the interview and reaffirm your interest and qualifications for the job

COMMON QUESTIONS ABOUT INTERVIEWING

What is the objective of an interview?
For the employer, it is to see if your paper image and portrayal stand up in real life: to see if you are a match for the position at hand. Your objective should be to explore whether or not this is a place you'd like to work. Formulate open-ended questions and probe. Look for indicators.

Do I have to dress up?
Yes, although more formal dress is usually most appropriate, gear yourself to the dress standards of the particular workplace. When in doubt, dress up to show you take the interview seriously.

How do I make an impression?
Be yourself. Smile. Use a firm handshake and make frequent eye contact. Elaborate on information from your resume that indicates you will work out well, that there is little risk in hiring you, and that you have a steady, predictable record of dedication. Be confident.

What should I bring?
Extra copies of your resume, and any other items that may be appropriate and relevant to the job. Be sure to provide these items at the proper point of the interview.

What is the best way to prepare?
List all the questions you think will be asked, talk to someone in the field or in a similar position, role-play with a friend or roommate, or any other activity that you feel will help you prepare.

How do I get information about the position or interviewer, or both?
Many firms are willing to send you a job description if you ask for one. It is possible to get a wealth of information about companies and even individuals on the Internet, or even from a library. College placement offices also have brochures, reports and other related information.

How do I get information during an interview?
You will always be given a chance to ask questions. Remember, though, that good interviewers will control the interview so that they first get all the information they want about you before they tell you too much about the job. In this way they avoid "telegraphing"—revealing the "right" answers to their questions.

How can I get them talking first?
After you answer a question, ask one. This will make the interview more conversational and natural. Ask open-ended questions like "In what direction is the company moving?" or "How would a typical day on the job be spent?"

What other techniques might the interviewer use?
If the interviewer has been trained well, he or she might "funnel" questions from general to specific—meaning they may begin by asking about general experience with customer service, followed by asking of any particular instances or bad experiences and how you handled them specifically.

How honest should I be?
Be honest, but not blunt. Don't offer negative information that is unnecessary or irrelevant. At the same time, you'll fit in best if you leave no surprises, especially about your abilities.

What if I'm asked a question I can't answer?
You more than likely will not be quizzed during your interview. A question that throws you can be handled by asking for clarification or an example, and if you still do not know, say so. However, too many "I don't knows" may indicate you failed to do enough preparation.

Will I be asked any trick questions?
Maybe. They will probably be concerned with how serious you are about this career, profession and particular job. They may ask about other alternatives or positions you may be considering, to which you want to appear as though you are focusing on this job exclusively. A common response by you may be, "Since this is exactly what I'm looking for, I've postponed looking at other positions. If I'm not accepted, I would probably check with (competitor)." Be aware that some employers have in mind certain answers or responses to certain questions that may disqualify you, so be careful how you field questions regarding future plans, other jobs, etc.

What should I ask about?
Whatever is necessary to meet your criteria for selection, and to give you a good feel for the job, the people and the working environment. Some topics to ask about are responsibilities, time commitments, co-workers, travel, style of management, the selection process, etc. Find out what your first day, week and month would be like on the job, and be able to explain how you would approach these responsibilities.

What questions will likely be asked?
The following is a list of common questions taken from interview evaluation forms and used frequently by many employers:

Why should I hire you?
What are your current job expectations?
Describe your educational background.
What was your favorite course in school? Why?
Describe the previous jobs you have had, beginning with your most recent.
What were your major responsibilities in your last job?
What are some of the things you did particularly well in your last job? Or achieved the greatest success in?
Why did you leave your last job?
What were some of the negative qualities of your last job?
What did you like most/least about your past jobs and academic work?
Describe something you did that was not normally part of your job.
Do you like working with figures?
What do you think are the qualities of a good supervisor?
What do you consider to be the perfect job for you?
What do you feel have been your most significant accomplishments?
Give an accurate description of yourself.
Would you have any trouble making it to work by 8:00 a.m.?
Describe what you see as your major strengths and weaknesses for the position.
Are there certain things you feel more confident about doing? What are they, and why do you feel the way you do?
If you had a choice of responsibilities within this department, which would you prefer?
How do you perceive your role in interacting with other department members?
What key factors attract you to this position or company?
What do you see yourself doing in five years?
How much independence and flexibility do you like in a job?
What do you expect for a starting salary?
When can you start?

TESTING

For some jobs, you may need to take a test. Usually, the job announcement or ad will say if a test is required. There are several types of selection and job fitness tests:

- Aptitude tests predict how easily you will learn the job and how well you perform job tasks
- Job knowledge and proficiency tests measure what you know and what you can do in a job (for example, word processing speed for a secretary job, knowledge of street names and routes for a firefighter job, etc.)
- Literacy tests measure reading and arithmetic levels
- Personality tests help identify your personal style in dealing with tasks and other people. Certain personalities can be well suited for some jobs and not so well suited for other jobs. For example, an outgoing person may be well suited for a sales job.
- Honesty and Integrity tests evaluate the likelihood of stealing and trustworthiness of applicants
- Physical ability tests measure strength, flexibility, stamina and speed for jobs that require physical performance
- Medical examinations and tests determine physical fitness to do a job
- Drug tests show the presence of illegal drugs that could impair job performance and threaten the safety of others

How to Prepare for Tests

You can't study directly for aptitude tests. But you can get ready to do your best by learning as much as you can about the test by taking other tests. Look for tests or quizzes in magazines and school books. Set time limits. By taking tests, you learn about the testing process. This will help you feel more comfortable when you are tested.

Brush up on your skills. For example, if you are taking a typing test, practice typing. If you're taking a construction test, review books and blueprints. Get ready for physical tests by doing activities similar to those required for the job. For literacy tests, review and do exercises in reading and math books or enroll in remedial classes.

It's natural to be nervous about tests (some anxiety may even help you). Here are some tips that will help you take most tests:

1. Make a list of what you need for the test (pencil, eyeglasses, ID, etc.) Check it before leaving.
2. Get a good night's sleep
3. If you're sick, call and reschedule the test
4. Leave for the test site early
5. If you have any physical difficulties, tell the test administrator
6. If you don't understand the test instructions, ask for help before the test begins
7. If there are strict time limits, budget the time. Don't linger on difficult questions.
8. Find out if guessing is penalized. If not, guess on questions you're not sure about.
9. If you have time, review your answers. Check to make sure you did not misread a question or make careless mistakes.
10. You may be able to re-take the test. Ask about the re-testing policy.
11. Get a proper interpretation of your scores. The scores may indicate other career opportunities that should be pursued.

AFTER THE INTERVIEW

Make each interview a learning experience. After it's over, ask yourself these questions:

- What points did I make that seemed to interest the employer?
- Did I present my qualifications well? Did I overlook qualifications that were important for the job?
- Did I learn all I needed to know about the job?
- Did I ask questions I had about the job?
- Did I talk too much? Too little?
- Was I too tense? Too relaxed?
- Was I too aggressive? Not aggressive enough?
- Was I dressed appropriately?
- Did I effectively close the interview?

Make a list of specific ways you can improve your next interview. Remember, "practice makes perfect" – the more you interview the better you will get at it.

If you plan carefully and stay motivated, you can "market your job talents." You will get a job that uses your skills and pays you well.

JOB SEARCH CHECKLIST

Complete Items 1-3 on the checklist before starting your job search
Complete items 4-5 every day of your search
Complete items 6-9 when you have interviews

1. Identify Occupations
    - Make a background and experience list
    - Review information on jobs
    - Identify jobs that use your talents

2. Identify Employers
    - Ask friends, relatives, etc. to help you look for job openings
    - Go to your State Employment Service Office for assistance
    - Contact employers to get company and job information
    - Utilize other sources to get job leads
    - Obtain job announcements and descriptions

3. Prepare Materials
    - Write resumes – use job announcements to match your skills with job requirements
    - Write cover letters or applications
    - Assemble a job search kit (pens, maps, guides, background list, etc.)
    - Use the Talent Bank

4. Plan Your Time
    - Wake up early to start looking for work
    - Make a "to do" list of everything you'll do to look for a job
    - Work hard all day to find a job
    - Reward yourself

5. Contact Employers
    - Call employers directly (even if they're not advertising openings)
    - Talk to the person who would supervise you if you were hired
    - Go to companies to fill out applications
    - Contact friends and relatives to see if they know about openings
    - Use America's Job Bank on the Internet

6. Prepare for Interviews
    - Learn about the company you're interviewing with
    - Review job announcements to determine how your skills will help you do the job
    - Assemble resumes, forms, etc.

7. Go to Interviews
    - Dress right for the interview – go alone
    - Be clean, concise, positive
    - Thank the interviewer

8. Evaluate Interviews
    - Send a hand-written thank you note to the interviewer within 24 hours
    - Think about how you could improve the interview

9. Take Tests
    - Find out about the test(s) you will be taking
    - Brush up on job skills
    - Relax and be confident

10. Accept the Job!
    - Understand job duties and expectations, work hours, salary, benefits, etc.
    - Be flexible when discussing salary (but don't sell yourself short)
    - Congratulations!

THE MOST COMMON JOB-HUNTING MISTAKES

1. Not taking action – Putting off decisions, phone calls, leads, writing, looking. Not doing anything constructive. Avoiding even thinking about doing something. Making excuses, limiting yourself, erecting roadblocks to progress, complaining and generally procrastinating.

2. Not reflecting enough – Not thinking about what is wanted, ideal or possible. Jumping to the search and jumping too often to the wrong job, simply because it appeared first.

3. Not taking advantage of all potential resources – Overlooking the assistance and leads that can be found in talking with friends, parents, professors, etc. Not using libraries or the Internet. Hesitating to call people you don't know.

4. Not exploiting skills and experience – Not understanding the unique value, strengths and marketability of your past.

5. Not being committed to the job search – Not making adequate time for preparing and searching, or not giving it the highest priority.

6. Not empathizing with the employer's perspective – The employer has needs, time frames, problems and constraints that may or may not be compatible with yours.

7. Not being positive – Underestimating the power of attitude on the process and the employer.

8. Not anticipating and practicing for an interview – Not being able to relate your abilities to the employer's needs. Not role-playing and formulating a strategy for success.

9. Not following up in a professional manner – Thank-you letters, even after rejection, can make a name for you in what may prove to be a small, closely knit profession.

Below, in rank order, are reasons business and industrial managers gave for not offering a job to a new graduate, based upon a survey by Frank S. Endicott, former Director of Placement of Northwestern University:

1. Poor personal appearance
2. Overbearing know-it-all
3. Inability to express self clearly; poor voice, diction, grammar
4. Lack of planning for career; no purpose or goals
5. Lack of confidence and poise
6. Lack of interest and enthusiasm
7. Failure to participate in activities
8. Overemphasis on money; interest only in best dollar offer
9. Poor scholastic record—just got by
10. Unwilling to start at the bottom—expects too much too soon
11. Makes excuses, evasiveness, hedges on unfavorable factors in records
12. Lack of tact
13. Lack of maturity
14. Lack of courtesy
15. Condemnation of past employers
16. Lack of social understandings
17. Marked dislike for school work
18. Lack of vitality
19. Fails to look interviewer in the eye
20. Limp, fishy handshake
21. Indecision
22. Loafs during vacations preferring lakeside pleasures
23. Unhappy married life
24. Friction with parents
25. Sloppy application blank
26. Merely shopping around
27. Only wants a job for short time
28. Little sense of humor
29. Lack of knowledge of field of specialization
30. Parents make decision for them
31. No interest in company or industry
32. Emphasis on who they know
33. Unwillingness to go where we sent them
34. Cynical
35. Low moral standards
36. Lazy
37. Intolerant with strong prejudices
38. Narrow interests
39. Spends much time in movies
40. Poor handling of personal finances
41. No interest in community activities
42. Inability to take criticism
43. Lack of appreciation of value of experience
44. Radical ideas
45. Late to interview without good reason
46. Never heard of company
47. Failure to express appreciation for interviewer's time
48. Asks no questions about the job
49. High-pressure type
50. Indefinite response to questions

COMMON QUESTIONS ABOUT THE FOLLOW-UP

How important is the thank-you letter?
Thank-you letters have been found to be the only correlation between people who are looking for positions and those who get hired. They've been found to correlate even more than qualifications, amount of experience or degree of interest.

What is involved in a good thank-you letter?
This is usually personal, explaining your interest in the position, referring to a topic which was discussed, or providing more indicators of how well you'll fit in. More information about your qualifications, an example of your work and alternative solutions to a problem which you learned of during the interview would all be appropriate. This letter serves to concisely remind them of you at the time of the employment decision.

When should I send it?
You should send a hand-written letter within 24 hours of the interview.

Is timing important?
Yes. Most job processes, including selections and applicant review, are RANDOM. The most qualified applicant is often buried beneath those who were a bit more aggressive and marketed themselves more effectively. Hence, the more leads you pursue, the greater chance of success.

How can I be persistent without being overbearing?
Proper follow-up is more a matter of the right timing, not the quantity of contacts. Ask when the decision is being made, or check back when you feel they've reviewed your resume or are making the hiring decision after your interview.

What should I do if I think I'm being stalled?
Employers often put an applicant on hold. This may be because they are waiting for final approval of the position or because they think they can attract more qualified applicants if they delay. You can force the issue subtly by alluding to another job offer, or you can be more blatant by giving a date by which you need to know. Either method indicates you have a sense of value and self-worth and are not willing to be put off. Be careful not to appear too demanding though.

I was rejected, but I have no idea why.
Chances are small that you'll ever be given the real reason. If you felt you had a good chance, you should persist and acquire information that can help you for your next interview.

AFTER YOU ARE HIRED

- Come to closure with hanging leads – Contact any employers who are still considering you and tell them you've found a job, and thank them for their interest. Regardless of the profession you choose, you can be certain it is a tight network. You may want to work for one of those employers later, or keep in contact with them in your current position.
- Learn to listen
- Learn the background of your area – The history of the people and the development of departmental responsibilities can help give you indicators of

the written and unwritten "rules" of the field, and what changes can be expected.

- Learn the informal power network – Bear in mind that power is often outside the formal structure. Who is respected and who is not? Whose opinion of you is going to matter more than anything you do?

- Make time for people as well as the task – Focus on doing a good job, but also be sure to concentrate on developing good relationships with those you work with. Both are important. Be sensitive to your place within the hierarchy.

- Be sensitive to processes – What may seem slow or inefficient might serve a valuable purpose that is not initially apparent. Learn through observing.

- Keep the right attitude and perspective – Be appreciative of the opportunity long after you are hired. No matter what may be asked of you, try to treat each assignment as a learning experience.

- Use your resources to their fullest potential – Take advantage of all the options available to you to learn in your current environment. Taking part in projects and committees can be beneficial and show you are interested. Learn all you can as soon as you can.